ENGLISH THROUGH TOPICS

WEATHER
KEY STAGE 1

TEACHER'S BOOK

Sue Palmer and Avril Barton

Oliver & Boyd

Acknowledgements

The authors would like to thank all those involved in the production of *English Through Topics 'Weather'* (Key Stage 1). We are especially grateful to Dee Brinton, Janet Weller, Jenny Hodgkins and Heather Richards; Carol Kimberley, Lilian Whitford, and other staff and pupils of Truro Nursery School; Steve Uttley, Marianne Jackson, Lucille Rayner and other staff and pupils of St Columb Minor Primary School, Newquay; Matthew Brinton, Sarah Eacott, Daniel Neave, Martin Ballard and Lee Burford, who did so much handwriting; Soraj Lal of the Lothian Racial Equality Council; all those people who gave us rhymes and stories, hummed tunes and otherwise provided us with resource material; Truro Library and Cornwall Schools' Library Service; the teachers and children all over Britain who reported on the pilot material; two long-suffering husbands; and, last but not least, Beth Brinton and Sally Barton.

We are grateful to the following for permission to reproduce copyright material:

The Controller of Her Majesty's Stationery Office for extracts from English in the National curriculum (1989) and Penguin Books Ltd for the poem 'A Windy Day' from Five Furry Teddy Bears by Linda Hammond. Copyright © Linda Hammond 1990, pubd. in Puffin Books, 1990.

We have unfortunately been unable to trace the copyright owner of the poem 'Water has no colour' by Ilo Orleans and would appreciate any information that would enable us to do so.

The 'Record-keeping checklists' on pages 15, 36 and 71 refer to the National Curriculum in English at the time of going to press (Autumn 1992). Updated checklists for the revised curriculum, when known, are available free to purchasing schools, from Oliver & Boyd, Longman House, Burnt Mill, Harlow, Essex CM20 2JE.

Oliver & Boyd

Longman House
Burnt Mill, Harlow
Essex CM20 2JE

An imprint of Longman Group UK Ltd

First published 1993
ISBN 0050 05064 8

© Oliver & Boyd 1993

All rights reserved: no part of this publication may be reproduced, stored in a retrieval system, or transmitted in any form or by any means, electronic, mechanical, photocopying, recording, or otherwise without the prior written permission of the Publishers or a licence permitting restricted copying in the United Kingdom by the Copyright Licensing Agency Ltd, 90 Tottenham Court Road, London, W1P 9HE.

Set in Cheltenham

Printed and bound by Bell and Bain Ltd., Glasgow

Designed and illustrated by Celia Hart

CONTENTS

General introduction	5
Book 1	
Introduction	13
Contents	17
Facsimiles of pupils' material/teacher's notes	18
Book 2	
Introduction	34
Contents	39
Facsimiles of pupils' material/teacher's notes	40
Extra material for storytelling/drama	64
Book 3	
Introduction	69
Contents	73
Facsimiles of pupils' material/teacher's notes	74
Extra material for prediction	107
Make a snowflake	109
Non-fiction books on weather	110
Programmes of Study for Key Stage 1, England and Wales	111
Programmes of Study for Scotland	115

GENERAL INTRODUCTION

What is ETT?

English Through Topics provides:
English resource material based on the National Curriculum English documents linked to the theme of Weather.

At Key Stage 1, the material is graded for three levels of ability, based on **National Curriculum Attainment Target Levels**:

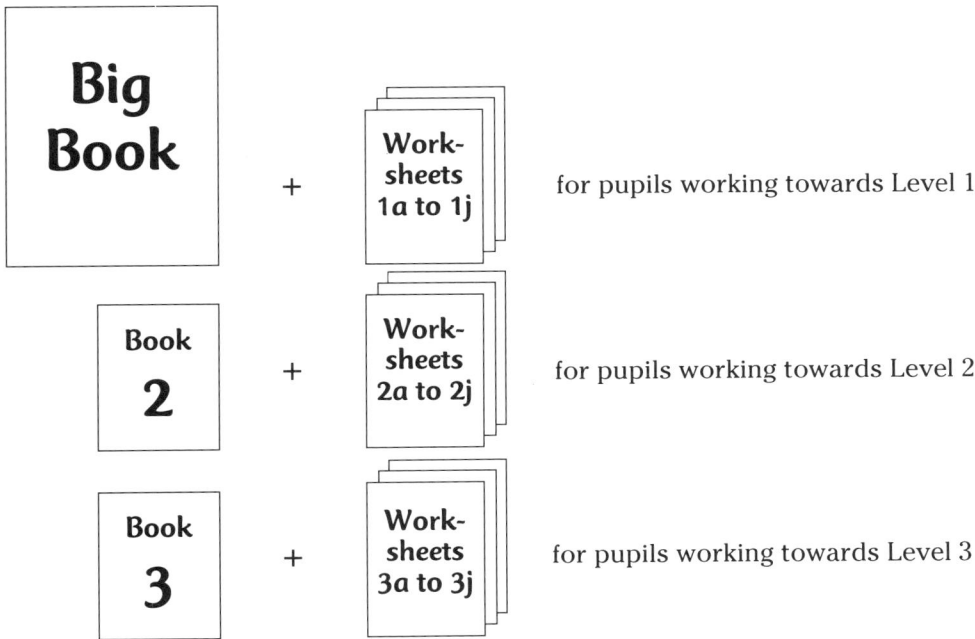

This Teacher's Book contains:
- detailed notes for each page of the pupils' books
- suggestions for teaching strategies
- additional resource material
- Notes for Big Book   pages 18 – 33
- Notes for Book 2   pages 40 – 66
- Notes for Book 3   pages 74 – 109

What ETT isn't

English Through Topics 'Weather' is not a topic pack. It does not provide detailed suggestions for activities in curricular areas other than English.

Fitting ETT into the school curriculum

English Through Topics 'Weather' is flexible:

At our school we like to keep the subject areas separate. But I do see the point of having a theme to provide a context for a term's work.

1 Use it as an integrated English course linked by a common theme.

Our school policy is to start with English work, and to exploit cross-curricular links wherever possible. It's good to make links but English should never be subordinated to other curriculum areas.

2 Use it as an integrated English course providing starting points for cross-curricular work on Weather.
- Science/Technology links are indicated throughout the Teacher's Notes.

We believe in cross-curricular teaching — integrating the subject areas need not mean you neglect anything. You just have to take care to cover all aspects of the English curriculum.

3 Use it as a ready structured English strand for a cross-curricular project on Weather or a related topic.

4 Even when not in use as a structured course, ETT 'Weather' is a useful resource for occasional reference.

English Through Topics is intended to supplement the ongoing literacy learning in the primary classroom. It assumes that children will, in addition to *English Through Topics*, have access to a wide range of fiction and non-fiction material within a structured reading and writing programme.

Using ETT in the classroom

English Through Topics provides resource material on the Weather theme for pupils at every developmental level in Key Stage 1, e.g.:

I've got a mixed infant class. Most of them are Level 1, working towards Level 2, but a few have reached Level 2.

Use Book 2 with the majority of the class, but supplement it with work from Book 3 for the post-Level 2 children.

Our school sets children for English by developmental level. All the children in my class are working towards Level 3.

Use Book 3 as a basic class text.

My class is a real mixture! Some aren't at Level 1 yet. Most are on the way to Level 2, and a few are already there and heading for Level 3.

Use Book 1 with the pre-Level 1 children, Book 2 with the majority of the class, and Book 3 with post-Level 2 pupils.

Using the Teacher's Notes

A reduced page(s) of the pupil's book is shown in the Teacher's Book. This is so that the teacher can see what the pupils are seeing, and at the same time check the relevant notes.

Organisation
In the margin are notes and suggestions for using the page, to cover particular areas of the English curriculum.

A brief explanation of the purpose of a resource or exercise.

Specific teaching targets

Notes are grouped, sometimes in boxes, to constitute one teaching session, one complete activity, or one unit of information.

Suggested questions for you to ask pupils and specific instructions are in *italics*.

Worksheets are linked to particular pages (these are listed on the first page of the introduction to each book).

Mrs Hippo's washing day *(page 6)*

This page provides discussion material about:
  story and story structure
  left – right sequencing
and a stimulus for individual children to explain parts of a story and retell a story to the teacher.

Work with small groups:
Ask the children to look carefully at the page. Help them to see the order in which the pictures should be read.

Science link: wind/drying conditions

Explaining/Retelling
What's happening in the first picture? And the second? etc.
What sort of weather is it in the story? Can anyone tell the whole story?

Story structure
How does the story begin/start?
What happens in the middle? How does it end?
Alternative phrasing: *What's the beginning? What's the ending?*
Do children understand all words in **bold** print?

Worksheet 1c: Sequencing/Following instructions
Explain:
the dotted lines show where to cut;
the pictures are muddled up;
the pupils have to stick them in the correct order.
Pupils require paste and paper on which to stick the cut-outs.

Give **two consecutive instructions**:
  First cut out the pictures.
  Then stick them in the correct order.
Pupils may also colour the worksheet. Some may be able to dictate a sentence to accompany each picture.
(See also **Worksheet 1j** – overlay for Concept Keyboard. A similar overlay could be made for the Mrs Hippo story and used as for Worksheet 1j.)

Picture books
The Wind Blew, Pat Hutchins (Picture Puffin)
Mrs Mopple's Washing Line, Anita Hewett and Robert Broomfield (Picture Puffin)
A Walk In The Wind, Rosemary Border (Macdonald)

Smaller text for notes to the teacher on things to watch out for when teaching *English Through Topics*.

At the foot of most pages is a list of fiction and/or non-fiction books or stories which relate to the material on the pupil's book page.

Where space permits, further poems, songs, folktales, etc. are included.

Possible links to N. C. Science and/or Technology are suggested where appropriate.

ETT 'Weather' at Key Stage 1

The Pupil's Books include:

- poems, songs, rhymes about weather

- stories, folktales and legends, plays and other fiction on the theme

- non-fiction writing, instructions for activities, and a variety of other types of text, such as signs, shopping lists, posters and letters related to aspects of weather

- starting points for drama, role-play, discussion, group work and presentations, and other spoken language activities, all related to the weather theme

- stimuli for writing activities – fiction and non-fiction, narrative and non-narrative – for a variety of purposes and audiences, linked to the theme.

The Teacher's Notes contain:

- suggestions for developing pupils' skills in speaking and listening, reading and writing, linked through the resource material to the weather theme

- suggestions for integrating teaching about language and the conventions of written English into children's work on the weather theme,
  e.g.:   *for pupils approaching Level 1*
               symbolic information, concepts of print
               and story, left-right sequencing
         for pupils approaching Level 2
               phonological awareness, significance of
               punctuation, sentences
         for pupils approaching Level 3
               metalinguistic terms,
               spelling and punctuation

- additional resource material, including further stories, rhymes, poems and songs linked to the theme

- details of children's picture books, story books and non-fiction suitable for use with each age-group

- the Programmes of Study for England, Wales and Scotand (see pages 111 – 118).

Using a Pupil's Book across one attainment band

The material in each pupil's book has been pitched about halfway between the Attainment Level pupils have already reached and that at which they are aiming.

Beginners
These are pupils who have only recently reached the previous attainment level.
Beginners need plenty of support, e.g.:
- help with reading and writing
- plenty of clear explanations
- help with activities and worksheets.

Midway pupils
These are pupils about halfway between levels. Midway pupils need teaching support but are more independent than beginners. For example, they can:
- read the stories alone
- complete activities and worksheets with occasional help.

Teachers should watch for areas where concepts and vocabulary need more practice.

Independent pupils
These are pupils who have almost reached the Level of Attainment by which the pupil's book is numbered.
Generally, they should be able to:
- read all texts with minimal help
- carry out activities independently.

Teaching help should now be:
- 'fine tuning'
- encouraging independence and preparing for transitions to the next level.

Assessment and record-keeping

Assessment
On the opposite page we outline the teaching input appropriate for children at various stages of development. Criterion-referenced assessment is the other side of this coin.

The resource material and teaching suggestions have been carefully matched to the National Curriculum Attainment Targets. Pupils' stage of development can be assessed informally through their performance on the suggested activities.

Included in the Introductory Notes for each stage in this Teacher's Book is a criterion-referenced assessment grid.

   Level 1 Assessment Grid – page 15
   Level 2 Assessment Grid – page 36
   Level 3 Assessment Grid – page 71

These grids give a general indication of what can be expected of children as they progress along the continuum of achievement within each Level of Attainment, e.g. at Level 2:

- Pupils who can work independently from the Big Book but require considerable support on Book 2 (see grid on page 15) are **Level 2 Beginner** pupils.
- Pupils who achieve satisfactory results with an average amount of teacher input (see grid on page 15) are **Level 2 Midway** pupils.
- Pupils who work competently with minimum support, but are not yet quite ready for Book 3 (see grid on page 15) are **Level 2 Independent** pupils.

English Through Topics has not been designed primarily for this purpose, but as **teaching** material.

Simplified versions of the three Assessment Grids are included in the Key Stage 1 Copymaster pack, for use as individual pupil assessment sheets. On these sheets, teachers may record the dates at which a pupil's performance on ETT material/activities indicates that s/he has reached particular stages of development (Beginner, Midway or Independent).

Record-keeping
Materials for recording details of individual pupils' progress are described above. You may also wish to keep a record of work undertaken in English with a class or group.

The Introductory Notes to each level of ETT include a checklist, correlating the activities for each page of the book with the National Curriculum English Attainment Targets. These pages are reproduced in the *Copymaster* pack for record-keeping purposes. Copies may be included in a teacher's Record of Work for English, to record the work undertaken through the medium of ETT by a particular class or group.

As the activities for each page of ETT are completed, the page number may be ticked off or highlighted on the record sheet. As a running record is built up, there will be clear indications of the areas where extra input is necessary.

The N. C. Attainment Targets are merely guides to pupils' overall performance. There are many elements of pupils' language development which are contributory factors to reaching each target, but which are not specifically mentioned.

The Big Book (Book 1)

Pupils working towards Level 1

THE BIG BOOK: resource material, linked to the theme of weather, of the following types:
- well-known rhymes and songs
- action rhymes
- simple picture stories
- picture stimuli for discussion
- pictures incorporating familiar 'environmental print'
- pictorial instructions for practical work.

TEACHER'S NOTES: accompanying each page of the Big Book:
- suggestions for using the resource material to cover Level 1 English requirements.
  (A guide to the layout of the Teacher's Notes is given on page 8.)
- more poems, rhymes and songs and stories
- details of picture books related to the theme for teachers to share with pupils.

WORKSHEETS: practice work for pupils on:
1a Pre-handwriting hand control	(link to Big Book page 3)
1b Recognition of environmental print	(link to page 4-5)
1c Sequencing	(link to pages 6)
1d Recognising significant detail	(link to page 7)
1e Categorisation/colour symbolism	(link to page 8-9)
1f Recognition of environmental print	(link to page 8-9)
1g Anti-clockwise hand movements	(link to pages 10)
1h Pre-handwriting hand control	(link to pages 12-13)
1i Using a concept keyboard	(link to page 15)
1j Looking for significant detail/copying	(general)

While detailed suggestions for the use of the resource material are provided, individual teachers have their own preferred methods of working, and should use the materials as is most appropriate to their own teaching styles and their pupils' needs.

Covering the English Curriculum

The material is intended to **supplement** the ongoing language work for children working towards Level 1 and link it to the theme of Weather.

The Big Book has been designed to provide:
- stimuli for group discussion, drama and imaginative play;
- opportunities for children to follow specific instructions;
- activities which will develop children's concepts of print, especially the significance of
    - symbolic information
    - context
    - words, letters, numbers
    - sequence and left – right tracking
    - sound/symbol correspondence
    - the visual features of words/letters;
- material which shows children that reading can be enjoyable, meaningful and productive;
- information about the basic structure of a story;
- activities to develop hand control and pencil movements appropriate for correct letter-formation (to supplement classwork in handwriting, linking it to the theme);
- opportunities to record information
    - pictorially
    - symbolically.

Links between the above and Science/Technology are indicated throughout the Teacher's Notes. There are also possible links to Art, Maths, Health Education, Information Technology, Music and Movement. It is left to the teacher to decide how far and in what ways to exploit these cross-curricular links.

Keeping track

The Record-keeping checklist on page 15 and the Record-keeping sheets in the *Copymasters* match the National Curriculum Attainment Targets for Level 1 with the activities suggested in these notes. The numbers used to record the correlations are the page numbers of the Pupil's Book against which activities are recommended in the Teacher's Notes.

Please see also the notes on page 11 about record-keeping.

Record-keeping checklist

Opportunities for covering Level 1 NC English Attainment Targets

	See activities suggested to accompany the pages given below in the Big Book:														
Speaking and Listening															
Speak/listen in group activities	2/3	4/5	6	7	8/9	10	11	12	13	14	15	16			
Speak/listen in imaginative play		4/5		7	8/9	10				14					
Listen/respond to stories			6								15				
Listen/respond to poems	2/3			7	8/9	10		12	13	14		16			
Respond to simple instructions	2/3	4/5	6	7	8/9	10	11	12	13	14	15	16			
Follow two consecutive instructions	2/3	4/5	6	7	8/9	10	11	12	13	14	15	16			
Reading															
Recognise that print carries meaning:															
in books	2/3	4/5		7	8/9	10	11	12	13	14	15	16			
in other forms		4/5			8/9		11			14	15	16			
Recognise words in familiar contexts	2/3	4/5		7	8/9	10	11	12	13	14	15	16			
Recognise letters in familiar contexts		4/5			8/9			12	13	14		16			
Show signs of interest in reading			Opportunities throughout												
Talk about the content of stories			6								15				
Talk about information in non-fiction						11						16			
Writing															
Communicate meaning through:															
pictures		4/5	6		8/9					14	15	16			
symbols or isolated letters		4/5			8/9	10					15	16			
words or phrases		4/5			8/9					14	15				
Spelling															
Recognise difference:															
drawing/writing		4/5			8/9						15	16			
numbers/letters		4/5			8/9						15				
Write letter shapes for speech sounds		4/5			8/9										
Write letter shapes for letter names									13						
Use single/groups of letters to represent words															
Handwriting															
Form letters with control	2/3					10		12							

This checklist refers to the National Curriculum in English at the time of going to press (Autumn 1992). An updated sheet for the revised curriculum, when known, is available free to purchasing schools, from Oliver & Boyd, Longman House, Burnt Mill, Harlow, Essex CM20 2JE.

Assessing and teaching children using ETT Book 1

(See notes on assessment in General introduction, page 11 and *Copymasters*, page ix)

The resource material is pitched for teaching purposes at a point just below a Level 1 standard. Teacher input will, of course, vary with each child's needs at each stage. Developmental progress can be assessed informally by observation of the child's performance when using the resource material and carrying out activities.
For example:

	Working towards Level 1	**Nearing Level 1**
Spoken English behaviour	Beginning to participate in group discussions and role-play situations; usually settling to listen to stories, rhymes, etc. and learning some of them; able to follow instructions with occasional guidance.	Participating confidently in group discussions and role-play situations; listening attentively to stories, rhymes, etc. and learning them easily; confidently following two consecutive instructions without help.
Reading behaviour	Showing some appreciation of the significance of environmental print; beginning to recognise some words/letters with help; beginning to participate in discussing stories/rhymes/activities; beginning to match words to pictures.	Responding to environmental print, often correctly, and remembering what signs say; recognising odd words/letters; participating confidently in discussions about stories/rhymes/activities; matching words to pictures confidently and usually successfully.
Writing behaviour	Completing worksheets with some support; attempting to write in response to some stories/rhymes.	Completing worksheets independently with success; attempting to write in response to stories/rhymes quite frequently.
Spelling behaviour	Beginning to distinguish between symbols/numbers/letters; beginning to recognise individual letter sounds; occasionally trying to use letters to make a word.	Always able to distinguish between symbols/numbers/letters; able to say why P stands for Parking and other initials for other words; able to select a few appropriate letters to represent words.
Handwriting behaviour	Able to complete hand-control worksheets with help.	Able to complete hand-control worksheets neatly and independently.

Contents

	Page no. in Big Book
The sun has got his hat on	3
Hot day at the beach	4
Mrs Hippo's washing day	6
The north wind doth blow	7
Cold day in the town	8
The snowman	10
Umbrella	11
Rain	12
Dr Foster	14
The foggy day	15
Our weather chart	16

'The sun has got his hat on' (pages 2 – 3)

The sun has got his hat on,
Hip, hip, hip, hooray.
The sun has got his hat on,
And he's coming out to play.

Discussion: rainbows

Discuss, relating to children's own experience, e.g. *Have you ever seen a rainbow? Where was it? Do you know any stories about rainbows?* (For example: the crock of gold supposedly buried at the rainbow's end, the rainbow sent after the Great Flood, etc.) *What sort of weather do rainbows happen in?* etc.

(There is also a Caribbean proverb: 'If you don't get the rain, how can you get the rainbow?')

Science link: observation, colour

Discussion: colours

Do the children know the names of all the colours of the rainbow?
(Accept 'purple' for indigo.)
Which is your favourite colour? Why? Which is your unfavourite colour? Why? What things can you think of that are red/orange/yellow/blue/green/violet/purple?

(Perhaps pupils could be encouraged to look out for items in the less familiar shades and bring them in for a display.)

Cooperative group work

Groups of children could compile rainbow stripes made up of red/orange/yellow/etc. things, each group contributing a single colour stripe (mixing paint, wax crayon, collage, etc.)

Song

This rhyme is part of the song 'The Sun Has Got His Hat On' from 'Me and My Gal' by Ralph Butler and Noel Gay, 1932. A recorded version is available on the EMI cassette, *20 All Time Junior Hits* - TC MFP 50488.

Rhyme

Red is for danger – so don't cross the street;
Orange for oranges, juicy and sweet;
Yellow, the daffodils bright as we pass;
Green is the colour of trees, leaves and grass;
Blue makes me think of a clear, cloudless sky;
Indigo's rich like a deep purple dye;
Violets are flowers, a soft pinky-blue;
I love to see bright rainbow colours – don't you?

(Sue Brinton)

Listening/Memory
Read or sing the rhyme several times with the children.

Discussion: the sun

Science links: light, radiation, colour; day/night; summer/winter; observation.

For example:
What colour is it?
What shape is it?
Where do we see it?
When do we see it? (day/night; summer/winter)
Why should you never stare at it?
What is the difference between the winter sun/the summer sun? etc.

Spoken language: following two consecutive instructions

Worksheet 1a
First explain how to join the dotted lines, starting at the large dot. Then give instructions:
Join up the dotted lines.
Then draw a hat on the sun.
Handwriting: hand control practice.

1a

Poem/Listening/Discussion

Another poem about hot weather, for reading to the children. After the first reading, they could join in with the 'and sit's.

> In summer when the days are hot
> I love to find a shady spot
> And hardly move a single bit
> Just sit
> and sit
> and sit
> and sit . . .
>
> (Anon.)

How does the sun make you feel? Why does it make some people feel lazy? How else can it make us feel? (e.g. thirsty, tired, sweaty)
What is the shade?
Why is it cooler there?

Science links: observation, changes caused by heat; light and shade.

Picture books
Once Upon a Rainbow, Gabrielle El Chenaur and Naomi Lewis (Cape)
A Walk In The Sun, Rosemary Border (Macdonald)
The Sun Shone All The Time, Boswell Taylor (University of London Press)
What The Moon Saw, Brian Wildsmith (OUP)

Hot day at the beach (pages 4 – 5)

Discussion
Work with small groups. Discuss the picture, relating it to children's own experience, e.g.: *Have you ever been to the beach? What did you do there? Is the weather always hot when you go to the beach?*
Discuss the weather in this picture, e.g. *How can we tell it's a hot day?*

> Science links: characteristics of hot weather; reporting observations; light and shadow.

Environmental print/Symbols and signs
Do the children understand the significance of symbols, e.g. on the toilet doors – *What do they mean? How do you know?*
Do the children recognise printed words? *Are there any **words** in the picture?*
Do they realise that words carry information? *What do you think the words are there for?*
For each sign: *What do you think this one says? Why do you think that? Have you seen a sign like this anywhere?*
Do the children recognise the significance of letters/letter sounds?
What does the P stand for? Why do you think the people who put the sign up chose a P to mean PARKING?

Drama/Role-play: hot day at the beach
Now or later:
Discuss going to the beach – the sort of clothes you wear, etc.
There are lots of activities set at the beach for children to mime, e.g. digging, building sandcastles, jumping in waves, splashing, eating an ice cream, sunbathing.
Individual role-play of hot weather feelings, e.g. *Show how you look when you're:*
   hot   tired   sweaty   thirsty
   when you are eating a melting ice cream,
   when the cold waves lap over your feet, etc.
Group role-play of a family on the beach.

> Science link: communicating observations

Group work/Role-play/Planning
Set up an ice cream van like the one on the beach. Make an ICE CREAM sign for across the top; an OPEN/CLOSED sign; posters to show the ice creams/lollies and their prices; a 'sandwich board'/ advertising stand with 'Walls Ice Cream' or something similar. (Incorporate as much environmental print as possible.)
Adventurous classes might even set up a 'sunny beach corner', with a beach shop, lifebelt, car park, blow-up paddling pool, beach clothes for children to change into, etc.

Environmental print

Worksheet 1b: **Matching printed signs** |1b|

Children should draw lines to match the signs around the edge of the worksheet with the signs within the picture. They will probably need help with this, at least in the early stages, and the more adult helpers there are available the better. The worksheet provides a useful focus for discussion about the function of environmental print. If this discussion can be with individual children, or in a small group, it will be particularly beneficial.

Environmental print in the school

With small groups of children, look for signs within the school (e.g. LIBRARY, QUIET PLEASE, NO SMOKING or NO DOGS signs, Boys' toilets, Girls' toilets, etc.). Discuss why particular signs are where they are. See if children can remember what it says when you point to a sign later. Can they find any signs which are the same as others elsewhere in the school?
(Note also if available: H for hot, C for cold on taps; S and P on salt and pepper pots.)

See later follow-up on 'Environmental print in and around school' described in the notes for 'Cold day in the town' (page 25 in these Teacher's Notes).

Picture books

Lucy and Tom at the Beach, Shirley Hughes (Picture Corgi)
The Bears Who Went to The Seaside, Suzannah Gretz (Picture Puffin)
Teddy At The Seaside, Amanda Davidson (Picture Lions)
Henry's Sunbathe, Rodney Peppe (Magnet)

Mrs Hippo's washing day (page 6)

This page provides discussion material about:
  story and story structure
  left – right sequencing
and a stimulus for individual children to explain parts of a story and retell a story to the teacher.

Work with small groups:
Ask the children to look carefully at the page. Help them to see the order in which the pictures should be read.

Explaining/Retelling

Science link: wind/drying conditions

*What's happening in the first picture?
And the second?* etc.
*What sort of weather is it in the story?
Can anyone tell the whole story?*

Story structure

*How does the story **begin/start**?
What happens in the **middle**? How does it end?*
Alternative phrasing: *What's the beginning? What's the **ending**?*
Do children understand all words in **bold** print?

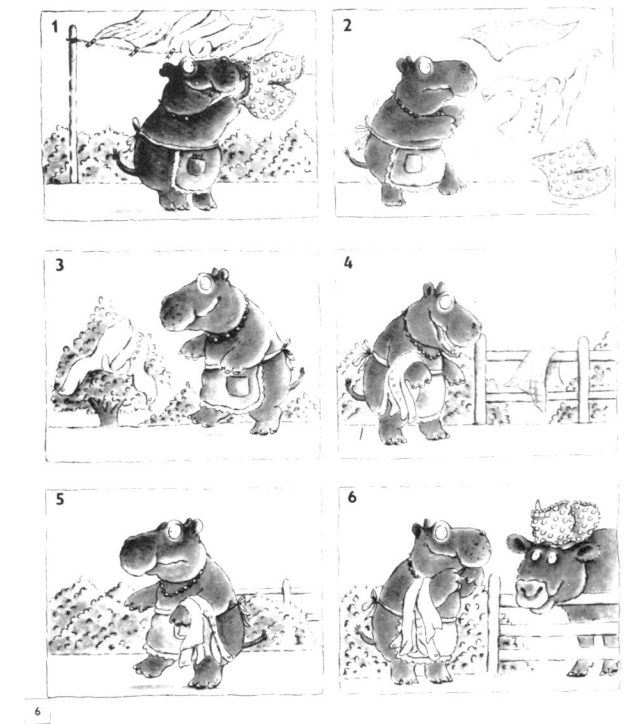

Worksheet 1c: Sequencing/Following instructions

Explain:
the dotted lines show where to cut;
the pictures are muddled up;
the pupils have to stick them in the correct order.

Pupils require paste and paper on which to stick the cut-outs.

Give **two consecutive instructions**:
  *First cut out the pictures.
  Then stick them in the correct order.*
Pupils may also colour the worksheet. Some may be able to dictate a sentence to accompany each picture.
(See also **Worksheet 1j** – overlay for Concept Keyboard. A similar overlay could be made for the Mrs Hippo story and used as for Worksheet 1j.)

Picture books

The Wind Blew, Pat Hutchins (Picture Puffin)
Mrs Mopple's Washing Line, Anita Hewett and Robert Broomfield (Picture Puffin)
A Walk In The Wind, Rosemary Border (Macdonald)

The North Wind doth blow (page 7)

The North Wind doth blow,
And we shall have snow,
And what will the robin do then?
Poor thing!
He'll hide in the barn,
To keep himself warm,
And hide his head under his wing,
Poor thing!

Discussion material/Action rhyme
1st verse only given in Big Book.
2nd and 3rd verses:

> The North wind doth blow,
> And we shall have snow,
> And what will the dormouse do then?
> Poor thing!
> Rolled up in a ball
> In his nest snug and small,
> He'll sleep till the winter is past,
> Poor thing.
>
> The North wind doth blow,
> And we shall have snow,
> And what will the children do then?
> Poor things!
> O, when lessons are done,
> They'll skip, jump and run,
> And play till they make themselves warm,
> Poor things.

Read the poem with the children and discuss it; e.g. explain that 'doth' is an old-fashioned version of 'does' so this must be a very old poem. *Do you really think the children are 'poor things'?* etc.

> Science links: warm and cold winds; different ways of keeping warm.

Discuss appropriate actions, then ask them to act out the poem a few times as you read it. Can children join in with the chorus lines?

Discussion: cold weather and animals

> Science links: animal behaviour – seasonal changes.

Verse 1: Animal shelters
What sort of home has the robin built in the barn? Where would other animals go for shelter?
(e.g. horse, cows, hedgehog, squirrel, rabbit, badger)
Verse 2: Animals that sleep in the winter
Why do some animals sleep all winter? Which other animals do you know of which do this? (e.g. toads, bears, hedgehogs, tortoises)
What do some birds do instead of sleeping or putting up with the weather?

Discussion: snowflakes
Do you know what a snowflake looks like under a microscope? etc.

> Science links: shape, size.

1d *Worksheet 1d*
Finding significant detail (snowflake pictures)

Books
Picture books:
One Snowy Night, Nick Butterworth (Collins)
Geraldine's Big Snow, Holly Kellar (Julia Macrae)

Story:
'What Will Little Bear Wear' from *Little Bear,* Elsie Holmelund Minarick (Puffin I Can Read)

Cold day in the town (pages 8 – 9)

Discussion/Environmental print/Recognition of symbols

Work with small groups.
Discuss the picture, relating it to the children's own experience, e.g. *Have you been to town in the snow? What was it/would it be like? How do people dress in cold weather?*
Have you got a coat with a hood/boots/woolly gloves, etc.?
What are the problems for traffic/old people in the snow?

Symbols and signs

Children should be more aware of these after the work on pages 4 – 5 and Worksheet 1b.
Symbol – man at work
Number on bus
Various signs – discuss each one, e.g. *Is the shop open or closed? Why does the lady have Tesco on her shopping bag? What does 'danger' mean?*
Single letter: L – do any children recognise its significance?

Drama/Role-play

Possible follow-up:
Getting dressed in warm clothes to go on a shopping trip.
Crossing the street in a busy town.

Discussion: summer and winter clothes

What sort of clothes do you need in winter/summer? How are they different? Why do you need different clothes in winter and summer? etc.

> Science links: heat and insulation; materials; seasonal changes.

Poem

A A Milne's 'If I Were A Bear and A Big Bear Too' in *Now We Are Six* (Puffin)

> **Worksheet 1e: Categorisation/Colour symbolism/Following instructions**
> Instructions should be given verbally, but the written versions pointed out and explained. Teachers could ask children to underline the word 'red' on the sheet in red and 'blue' in blue.

1e

Rhyme/Drama

This rhyme is suitable for inventing actions:

> This is how snowflakes play about,
> Up in cloudland they dance in and out.
>
> This is how they whirl down the street,
> Powdering everybody they meet.
>
> This is how they come fluttering down,
> Whitening roofs, and cars, and town.
>
> This is how people shiver and shake,
> On snowy mornings when first they wake.
>
> This is how snowflakes melt away
> When the sun sends out his beams to play.
>
> (Anon.)

Science link: communicating observations

Books

Picture books:
The Snowy Day, Ezra Jack Keats (Picture Puffin)
Sally Ann In The Snow, Petronella Breinburg (Bodley Head)
Bundle Up, Ann Morris (Heinemann)
Story:
'Bad Harry and the Milkman', from *My Naughty Little Sister's Friends*, Dorothy Edwards (Puffin)

Environmental print   1f

***Worksheet 1f:* matching printed signs**
As on Worksheet 1b, children should draw lines to match the signs around the edge of the worksheet with the signs within the picture.
Discussion, with individuals or small groups, will again be very valuable.

Environmental print in and around school
Do pupils remember the meaning of signs and symbols around the school (best of all, do they remember signs verbatim)?
With small groups, look for signs in the neighbourhood of the school – a local shopping area which the children often visit is ideal. Point out the common signs, e.g. FOR SALE, road signs, and ones which the children have met in our illustration, e.g. Bus Stop.
Can they find several examples of the same sign?

Note also H for hydrants, P for parking, L for learner, etc.

The snowman (page 10)

Action rhyme/Memorisation/Sequencing actions and words

Read the poem a few times and explain the actions. The combination of actions with words aids memorisation.

It is worth keeping an eye on those children who do not learn such rhymes easily or verbatim (especially if, in paraphrasing them, they lose the rhyming words). Such children may have difficulties with hearing (possibly intermittent hearing loss), which have made them less sensitive to sound than the average, or they may have poor auditory memory. If so, they will need particular help with phonological awareness when learning to read.

Discussion

Discussion of snowmen, relating to children's own experience, e.g. *Have you ever made a snowman? How long did it last? What happened to it? Why?* etc.
Discussion of snow, e.g. *What's it like? How does it affect us?* etc.

(Science link: melting snow (change))

Drama/Role-play

Playing in the snow - mime and movement to depict:
getting dressed in warm clothing, playing in the snow, making and throwing snowballs, making a snowman, feeling cold, coming in and warming up.

(Science link: body parts)

Discussion

Which parts of your body feel the cold most? How do your fingers/toes feel when they're very cold? How can you warm them up? etc.

Discussion/Planning and reflection

Provide a variety of materials suitable for making snowmen. Discuss with pupils as they choose (e.g. *What are you going to use? Why do you choose that?* – characteristics of materials) and as they work (*What are you doing? How are you going to stick it? How could you make it better?* etc. – decision making, awareness of process.)

(Technology link)

Handwriting 1g

Worksheet 1g
Anticlockwise patterns (Worksheet 1d is also appropriate to this page).

Picture books

The Snowman, Raymond Briggs (Hamish Hamilton)
Sophie and Jack in the Snow, Judy Taylor (Picture Corgi)
About melting: *Ice Cream*, Paul Dowling (Picture Lions)

Umbrella *(page 11)*

Following instructions/Sequencing

Children require:
- drinking straws
- Blutack or similar
- scissors
- thin card
- felt tips/crayons.

This activity is a fairly simple one. It should be possible for small groups of children to carry it out from the picture-instructions, provided they have been suitably briefed and help is available if needed.

Preparation:
- Talk the children through the picture-instructions, making sure they understand the order of the pictures (the left – right layout mimics print).
- Depending on the ability of the children, the umbrella shape can be provided ready drawn on card, or they can draw their own using a template.
- One possible method of organisation would be to start the children on the activity in staggered groups (while others are engaged on worksheets, e.g. Worksheet 1h, or other activities).

Discussion

Can you think of other ways of making umbrellas? (other materials/designs?)

Have you got a real umbrella? etc. *Can you explain how it works?* (You could look at one to work it out.)

(Technology link)

(Science link: forces)

Picture book

Miranda's Umbrella, Val Biro (Blackie)

Song

See back cover rhyme: 'Pray open your umbrella'. Music for this is as follows:

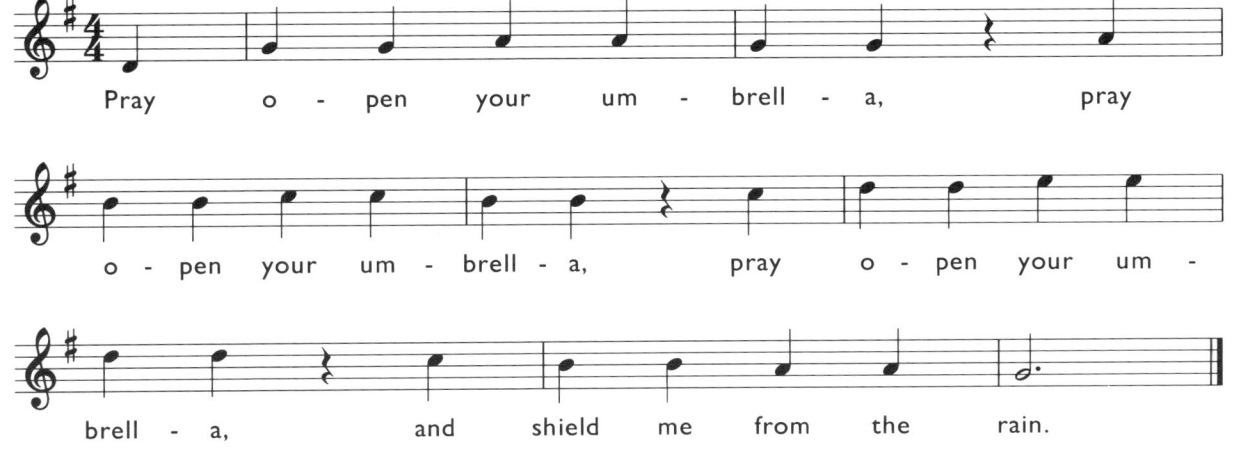

Pray o-pen your um-brell-a, pray o-pen your um-brell-a, pray o-pen your um-brell-a, and shield me from the rain.

27

Rain

Some children will probably know at least some of these rhymes about rain, and can join in from the start.

Discussion
General discussion of rain, relating it to children's own experience, e.g. *Do you like rain? What does it feel like? What sounds does the rain make?* (e.g. plip plop, splish splosh, drip drop, pitter patter – see Book 2, page 21)

> Science links: rain, sounds, effects of rain on materials/landscape.

What sort of clothes do we need in the rain? Where does rain go? Where does it come from? What do you think of thunder/lightning? Have you ever been in a storm?
Various versions of 'Rain, rain' and 'It's raining, it's pouring' and other 'rain-banishing spells' exist (e.g. in the West Indies: 'Rain, rain, go to Spain, Don't come back to Trinidad again'). Do the children know any others? *Why do people want the rain to go away? Why do we need rain?*

> Science link: water and life (importance for plants and animals)

Word recognition
The word 'rain' occurs several times on these pages (including appearances as part of 'raining' and 'raindrops') and probably elsewhere in the classroom. Can the children spot them all?

Print and meaning/Left – right tracking
Point to the words as you read the rhymes, matching printed words to spoken words. After a few goes at 'Rain Rain', ask the children to recite without your help, as you point. Try with 'It's raining, it's pouring'.

'Spot the word'
Next explain that, as you point, you are going to stop suddenly part way through the poem. Who can tell you which word your finger stops at? Try a few times, using 'Rain rain' first.

(page 12)

Poem for performance
'I hear thunder'
This poem can be sung as a round to the tune of 'Frère Jacques'.
Actions:
first line – stamp feet for thunder;
second line – hand to ear, to signify listening;
third line – hands descend with fingers wiggling to signify raindrops;
fourth line – point to self, point to someone else.
Percussion instruments could be used to provide an accompaniment. *What do you think would make the best sound to go with the thunder? the raindrops?* etc.

> Science link: sound production

Handwriting
Worksheet 1h
Practice of downward pencil movements.

1h

(page 13)

Rhythm and rhyme
Another rain poem with an excellent rhythm is:

> Marching in our wellingtons,
> Tramp, tramp, tramp.
> Marching in our wellingtons,
> We won't get damp!

Children can either march to this or, more sedately, bang out the marching rhythm on their knees, using alternate hands. A difficult but satisfying rendition can be achieved if one group chants 'Tramp tramp tramp' all the way through the poem.

Science link: sound production

Poem
'Happiness' ('John had Great Big Waterproof Boots On') in *When We Were Very Young*, AA Milne (Puffin)

Action rhyme

Incy Wincy spider climbed the water spout –	(action: see below)
Down came the rain and washed the spider out;	(downward motion of hands)
Out came the sun and dried up all the rain,	(upward motion of hands)
So Incy Wincy spider climbed the spout again.	(action: see below)

The traditional action for Incy Wincy climbing the spout is: forefinger of right hand touching tip of left thumb, forefinger of left hand touching tip of right thumb; move bottom finger/thumb up to top, and so on.

There is some evidence that left/right alternating movements of this kind may be useful in preparing children for types of mental activity involved in reading.

Science link: observation of weather changes

Discussion: sun and rain
What happens to rain water when the sun comes out? Why? Where does the water go? Where does the rain come from? etc.

Picture books
It Always Rains For Jackie, Ruth Corrin (Oxford)
Norah's Ark, Ann and Reg Cartwright (Picture Puffin)
Rain, Peter Spier (Collins) - pictures only
Rain, Peggy Blakeley (A & C Black)

Dr Foster

(page 14)

Again this poem is likely to be familiar to many children, and may be used for the 'Spot the word' game (see 'Print and meaning/Left – right tracking' for page 12).

Environmental print

Triangular sign:
What do you think it says?
Have you seen the '!' symbol before?
What do you think it means?
Rectangular sign:
Can you remember what the big word says? Have you ever seen a sign that says 'Welcome to…' (or 'Welcome' on a door mat)? Is there a 'Welcome to…' for your city/town/village?
What is Dr Foster's job? What is your doctor called?
(Maybe children have seen 'Dr' or 'Doctor' signs at the surgery, 'Hospital', 'Ambulance', the red cross symbol, etc.)

Capital/Lower case letters

The word 'Gloucester' occurs twice on the page: once in lower case and once in capitals. Do children know there are 'big letters' and 'little letters'? Can they find any other examples of 'big letters' on this page? On any other pages?

Word recognition

Can they find the word 'rain' on this page? (Refer: Teacher's Notes to page 12.)

Drama

As children say the poem, one child can be Dr Foster, walking along and falling into a puddle (all say 'SPLASH!'). A bag and umbrella help the actor get into role.

Activity/Discussion: rain and puddles

Take the children outside on a rainy day and let them experience the rain at first hand.
What does it taste/feel/sound like? What colour is it? (see poem in Teacher's Notes to Book 2, page 15) *What effect does it have on the soil/ the playground/your clothes/your skin?* etc.

Try stepping in puddles of varying depths!
What sounds does it make? What happens to the water? What happens to the mud?
(See poem in Book 3, page 25.)

Back in the classroom, use some of the words they have given on a 'Rain and puddles' poster.

Science links: observation, description; the senses; sounds.

Story book

Story about getting wellington boots off: 'The New Joke' in *Carrot Tops,* Joan Wyatt (Young Puffin)

The foggy day *(page 15)*

Sequencing/Left – right tracking
Work with small groups.
Remind pupils of the Mrs Hippo story on page 6 of the Big Book. Can they show you which order the pictures of this story are in?

Explaining/Retelling
What's happening in the first picture? And the second? etc.
Why did the mix-up happen? etc.
Can anyone tell the whole story?

Story structure
*How does the story **begin/start**?*
*What happens in the **middle**? How does it **end**?*

Discussion
Have you ever been out in the fog?
How can fog be dangerous? etc.

> Science links: observation; effects of weather.

Worksheet 1i: concept keyboard
This 'worksheet' is an A4 overlay for a concept keyboard. If another size is required, it could be enlarged or reduced on a photocopier.
Make the grid planner, as shown below.

Grid planner for Prompt/Writer
(MESU, University of Warwick)

Work with a small group. Tell children that the little boy's name is Tom.
Using the concept keyboard, ask children to press each picture in turn to display the written version of the story on the monitor, and to press COPY to print it. e.g. frame 1:
What do you think this says? (Guide children to the correct version.)

> Science link: information technology

Matching writing to pictures (possible follow-up to *Worksheet 1i*)
Each pupil (or pair of pupils) should have a worksheet and a print-out from the concept keyboard. They can colour and cut out the pictures, and stick them on to a larger sheet with the correct written text beside them. Adult help will probably be required to match pictures with writing.

Our weather chart *(page 16)*

Discussion
About the chart, e.g. *What do you think the chart in this picture is for? What tells you the days of the week? How does the chart show its is sunny/rainy/ etc.?*

Sequencing: days of the week
By this stage, most children should be able to recite the days of the week in sequence, or to learn them quite easily with rhythmic chanting.

Watch out for the child who finds it difficult to learn the days of the week - it may indicate sequencing difficulties or poor auditory memory, which can result in problems with literacy skills.

Discuss the days, e.g. *What's special about a Monday, Tuesday,* etc.?
Talk about the meaning of 'yesterday' and 'tomorrow'. *What was the weather like yesterday?* Keeping a weather chart can be a useful focus for developing children's awareness of the days of the week.

Symbols: making a class weather chart

Science link: communicating observation

Devise simple symbols for each type of weather appropriate to the season.

Cooperative work/Recording
Make a chart on a large piece of card and cover with sticky-back plastic. Children (in groups) can make weather symbols on card, which can be cut out and stuck with Blutack around the outside of the chart. (If cutting out of symbols is too difficult, use equally sized squares with picture on.)

My weather chart	
Monday	Tuesday
Wednesday	Thursday
Friday	Saturday
Sunday	Best day

As well as keeping a class weather chart in this way, pupils could keep weather diaries themselves (basic worksheet as shown; child copies weather symbol on each day). 'Best day' section encourages a review of the week's weather.

Rhyme
Whether the weather be cold,
Or whether the weather be hot:
We'll weather the weather,
Whatever the weather,
Whether we like it or not.

Finding significant detail/Copying shapes
Worksheet 1j
Discussion of different sorts of weather.

Picture books
Different sorts of weather:
Weather, Jan Pienkowski (Picture Puffin)
Weather and days of the week:
Mr Wolf's Week, Colin Hawkins (Picture Lions)
Other picture books featuring days of the week:
The Very Hungry Caterpillar, Eric Carle (Picture Puffin)
On Friday Something Funny Happened, John Prater (Bodley Head)

Book 2

Pupils working towards Level 2

Beginning independent reading and writing

PUPIL'S BOOK 2: resource material, linked to the theme of Weather, of the following types:
- poems and rhymes, many focusing on phonological aspects of language
- stories and a play with limited text, natural repetition, and strong pictorial support
- picture stimuli for discussion and activities, featuring 'environmental print'
- examples of different written texts, print styles and handwriting
- simple factual material
- instructions, combining pictures and print
- games relating to the alphabet and letter sounds.

THE TEACHER'S NOTES: accompanying the pages from the Pupil's Book:
- suggestions for using the resource material to cover Level 2 English requirements. (A guide to the layout of the Teacher's Notes is given on page 8.)
- further poems, rhymes and songs
- a folk story and a fable for the teacher to read aloud
- details of children's books on a weather theme which pupils can read for themselves at Level 2/3
- details of children's books and stories for the teacher to read to pupils (we call these 'Read aloud' books).

WORKSHEETS: practice work for pupils on:
2a Handwriting patterns   (link to Pupil's Book 2 pages 2-3)
2b Prediction   (link to page 4)
2c Matching handwritten and printed lists   (link to page 6)
2d Categorisation (the seasons)   (link to page 7)
2e Fiction/non-fiction   (link to page 8)
2f The alphabet   (link to page 12)
2g Sequencing/matching text to pictures   (link to page 14)
2h Simple sentence punctuation   (link to page 19)
2i Phonological awareness/phonic decoding   (link to page 21)
2j Reading/writing weather sentences (riddles)   (link to page 24)

While detailed suggestions for the use of the resource material are provided, individual teachers have their own preferred methods of working, and should use the materials as is most appropriate to their own teaching styles and their pupils' needs.

Covering the English curriculum

This material is intended to **supplement** the ongoing English activities for children working towards Level 2 and link them to the theme of Weather.

Pupil's Book 2 has been designed to provide:
- stimuli for discussion, drama, and various group activities, which involve using language for cooperative endeavour and following complex instructions;
- opportunities to listen and respond to poetry, fiction and non-fiction writing;
- opportunities to use spoken language in a wide variety of ways, including giving simple instructions;
- activities to develop pupils' growing understanding of the nature of print and their ability to bring meaning to it, developing:
    - sight vocabulary
    - context and picture cueing techniques
    - recognition of environmental print
    - letter recognition
    - sound/symbol association (initial letters and blends);
- activities designed to develop phonological awareness;
- recognition of the importance of print, in holding and conveying meaning in a wide variety of circumstances, for information and for pleasure;
- knowledge of the alphabet, alphabetical order, alphabet names and letter sounds;
- developing recognition of story structure, and opportunities to predict story endings on the basis of what has gone before;
- stimuli for a variety of simple writing activities, fiction and non-fiction, chronological and non-chronological;
- opportunities to look at the basic conventions of written English;
- opportunities to distinguish between fiction and non-fiction material.

Links between the above and Science and Technology are indicated throughout the Teacher's Notes. There are also possible links to Art, Information Technology, RE, Music and Movement. It is left to the teacher to decide how far and in what ways to exploit these cross-curricular links.

Keeping track

The Record-keeping checklist on page 36 and the Record-keeping sheets in the *Copymasters* match the National Curriculum Attainment Targets with the activities suggested in these notes. The numbers used to record these correlations are the relevant page numbers of Pupil's Book 2. (The activities concerned are actually described in the Teacher's Notes accompanying each page, but we found the Pupil's page numbers were easier for teachers to find/recall.)

Please see also the notes on page 11 about record-keeping.

Record-keeping checklist

Opportunities for covering Level 2 NC English Attainment Targets

See activities suggested to accompany the pages given below in Pupil's Book 2

Speaking and Listening													
Speak/listen in group activity	2/3	4/5	6/7	8/9	10	11	12	13	14	15	16–19	20	21	22–4	BC	TB66–8
Describe an event		4/5	6/7	8/9		11		13						24		TB66–8
Listen to/talk about stories/poems	2/3	4/5	6/7				12	13		15	16–19	20	21	22–4		TB66–8
Talk, discuss with teacher	2/3	4/5	6/7	8/9	10	11	12	13	14	15	16–19	20	21	22–4	BC	TB66–8
Respond to complex instructions	2/3	4/5	6/7	8/9			12	13	14		16–19	20	21	22–4	BC	TB66–8
Give simple instructions											16–19					
Reading																
Read/understand signs, labels, notices			6/7			11			14			20			BC	
Know alphabet					10		12									
Use word books, dictionaries	2/3	4/5	6/7	8/9	10	11	12	13	14		16–19	20	21	22–4	BC	
Use picture and context cues	2/3	4/5	6/7	8/9	10	11	12	13	14		16–19	20	21	22–4	BC	
Use sight words	2/3	4/5	6/7	8/9	10	11	12	13	14		16–19	20	21	22–4	BC	
Use phonic cues		4/5									16–19			22–4		
Describe what has happened in a story		4/5				12										
Predict what will happen next		4/5												22–4		
Listen/respond to stories	2/3	4/5	6/7	8/9				13		15	16–19		21	22–4		TB66–8
Listen/respond to poems			6/7	8/9	10	11	12	13	14		16–19	20		22–4	BC	
Independently read a range of material	2/3	4/5	6/7	8/9	10	11	12	13	14		16–19	20	21	22–4	BC	
Writing																
Produce writing in complete sentences		4/5	6/7	8/9		11		13	14		16–19			24		
Sometimes use cap/full stop/question mark			6/7	8/9		11		13	14		16–19			24		
Structure chronological accounts	2/3	4/5	6/7	8/9		11			14	15						
Write stories with story structure		4/5							14							
Simple non-chronological writing			6/7	8/9	10	12					16–19	20		22–4		
Spelling																
Produce recognisable spellings for common words	2/3	4/5	6/7	8/9		11		13	14			20	21	22–4		
Know/use some common regular patterns	2/3	4/5	6/7	8/9		11		13	14			20	21	22–4		
Apply regular patterns in unknown words		4/5	6/7	8/9		11			14	15		20		22–4		
Know names and order of alphabet		4/5			10				14							
Handwriting																
Produce legible upper/lower case letters		4/5	6/7	8/9		11			14			20		22–4		
Correct formation/orientation/with ascenders and descenders	2/3	4/5														

This checklist refers to the National Curriculum in English at the time of going to press (Autumn 1992). An updated sheet for the revised curriculum, when known, is available free to purchasing schools, from Oliver & Boyd, Longman House, Burnt Mill, Harlow, Essex CM20 2JE.

Assessing and teaching children using ETT Book 2

This material is pitched for teaching purposes at a point about halfway between Level 1 standard and Level 2 standard. Teacher input will, of course, vary to accommodate each child's needs as s/he progresses from 'beginner' to 'midway' to 'independent' (see General introduction, page 10). Therefore, discussion of assessment of children using the material is in many ways the obverse of discussion of teaching requirements (as discussed on page 11).

Developmental progress can be informally assessed by observation of the child's performance when using the resource materials and carrying out activities. For example:

	Just about Level 1 (beginner)	**About halfway between Levels 1 and 2** (midway)	**Nearing Level 2** (independent)
Speaking and listening	Needs supervision/support to complete group activities; needs direction in reporting/describing; lacks confidence in talking about stories/poems; needs support in following complex instructions for activities; unable to give simple instructions.	Gaining in confidence in group activities; beginning to report/describe clearly; beginning to talk about characters in stories/poems and to express preferences; gaining confidence in following complex instructions for activities and giving instructions to peers.	Able to complete group activities with little support; reporting/describing clearly; talks confidently about the stories and poems; able to follow complex instructions for activities and giving simple instructions to peers.
Reading	Needs help to read environmental print pages; unsure of alphabet; needs help to use picture/context/phonic cues; small sight vocabulary; needs help with prediction; does not read independently for pleasure.	Becoming more confident in reading environmental print pages; learning alphabet; beginning to use a variety of cues; sight vocabulary expanding; beginning to make predictions about stories based on what has gone before; showing more interest in books.	Reads environmental print pages independently; knows alphabet; using a variety of cues and sight vocabulary; good predicting skills based on knowledge of stories; beginning to read for pleasure without support.
Writing	Lacking confidence in writing own stories; little or no punctuation; stories lack coherent structure; unsure how to write lists, captions, tickets, programmes, etc.	Gaining in confidence in writing stories; appreciates the function of basic punctuation when reading; stories beginning to show some structure; more confident in tackling lists, captions, tickets, programmes, etc.	Writes stories with some punctuation; stories written with chronological structure, characters and one or more events; able to write lists, captions, tickets, etc.
Spelling	Unsure how to spell at all; needs support in order to attempt any spelling; does not know alphabet.	Beginning to try words independently; showing understanding of sound – symbol correspondence and simple regular spelling patterns; acquiring a small spelling vocabulary of words commonly used in the project.	Confident to try words using phonic knowledge; able to spell words with simple regular spelling patterns and words commonly used in the project; knows the alphabet.
Handwriting	Inconsistent size, shape; unsure of upper and lower case.	Developing control over size, shape of letters; knows the upper and lower cases; starting to keep writing on the line.	Writes clearly and with control over shape, size, case and orientation of letters; keeps to line.

Contents

Page in
Pupil's Book 2

All sorts	2
Claire's clouds	4
Holiday shopping	6
Sun out – rain in	8
What shall I wear today?	10
The school outing	11
One foggy day	12
Brrrr!	13
Making a snowstorm	14
Snow	15
The wind who wanted to play	16
Kite display	20
Rain	21
Guess what's outside	22
In the rain	24
Weatherwise	back cover
Folktales for storytelling/drama	Teacher's Notes only

All sorts

Poems/Discussion
Read the poems to the children a few times. Discuss them generally, relating to the children's own experience, e.g. *What sorts of weather do you like/dislike? Why?*
When the children have heard the poems several times: *Which poem do you like best/least, and why?*

Reading
When the children are familiar with the poems, they can help with the reading/reciting. Poems can be divided up, e.g.:
'Little wind' – 4 readers, 1 line each
'August Afternoon' – 6 readers, 2 lines each
'Thunderstorm' – teacher reads lines 1, 4 and 5 of each verse; all pupils join in with lines 2 and 3
'Understanding' – 6 readers, 1 line each.
(The teacher should re-read each poem again once children know which bits they are responsible for, so that they can familiarise themselves with the words.)

(page 2)

Little wind

Little wind, blow on the hill-top,
Little wind, blow down the plain;
Little wind, blow up the sunshine,
Little wind, blow off the rain.

Kate Greenaway

August Afternoon

Where shall we go?
What shall we play?
What shall we do
On a hot summer day?

We'll sit in the swing.
Go low. Go high.
And drink lemonade
Till the glass is dry.

One straw for you,
One straw for me,
In the cool green shade
Of the walnut tree.

Marion Edey and Dorothy Grider

Language
'Little Wind'
Each line of 'Little Wind' starts with the same words. What are they?
The poet asks the wind to blow **on**, *to blow* **down**, *to blow* **up**, *and to blow* **off** *– demonstrate each with a tiny piece of paper on your desk (Greenaway's version of 'blow up' not the usual one!). Where else can you blow?* (in/out/over/through, etc.)

Rhyme
'August Afternoon'
What does 'rhyme' mean? (Words with the same sound at the end)
Look at the rhymes – play/day; high/dry; me/tree. Can you think of other words that rhyme with each pair?
Read the poem again, emphasising the rhyming words. Then again, asking pupils to follow in their books and join in (loudly!) just on 'day', 'dry' and 'tree'.

(page 3)

> **THUNDERSTORM**
>
> I like to see a thunder storm,
> A dunder storm,
> A blunder storm,
> I like to see it, black and slow
> Come stumbling down the hills.
>
> I like to hear a thunder storm,
> A plunder storm,
> A wonder storm,
> Roar loudly at our little house
> And shake the window sills!
>
> Elizabeth Coatsworth

> **Understanding**
>
> Sun
> and rain
> and wind
> and storms
> and thunder go together.
>
> There has to be a little bit of each to make the weather.
>
> Myra Cohn Livingston

Handwriting
Worksheet 2a
This worksheet is intended only as a supplement to pupils' ongoing handwriting practice.

2a

Picture books
Windy weather: see books listed for Book 1, page 6; Book 2, page 19.
Hot weather: see books listed for Book 1, page 3.
Also *Hot Hippo,* Mwenye Hadithi (Hodder & Stoughton)
Thunderstorm:
The Big Storm, Christine Pullein-Thomson (Hodder & Stoughton)
Bringing The Rain to Kapiti Plain, V Aardama (Macmillan)

Sounds and rhymes
'Thunderstorm'
Enjoy the poem first, especially the rhythm and rhyme. Ask children for the three rhyming words in each verse – thunder, dunder, blunder; thunder, plunder, wonder – and write on board. *What do they mean?*
Look at the pattern of the spelling – like the pattern of the sounds, the words look the same at the end (shame about the 'o' in 'wonder' but this is English!)
The beginnings, however, are different. Can children separate out d-under, bl-under, th-under, etc. and hear the initial blends followed by rhymes, as you point to them on the board? Collect other words associated with thunder and lightning (e.g. BANG, BOOM, ZIG-ZAG, FLASH, CRASH). Can the children help spell them by their sounds? They could be displayed on a class collage of a thunderstorm.

Science link: sound

Discussion
'Understanding'
What sorts of weather do you like/dislike? Why do we need sun/rain/wind? Do we need thunderstorms for anything? Would you like to have 'good' weather all the time? What are your reasons for saying you would/wouldn't?

Science links: effects of weather; necessity for water to sustain life.

Claire's clouds

(page 4)

(Readability: Level 1+)

Sharing a story
The story is intended to be read with a group of children in the same way that you would read a simple picture book.

Predicting an ending
What do the '?' signs mean? Discuss with the children what they think will happen next. Elicit as many responses as possible: *Is Claire frightened or excited or . . .? What might she do next?*
With each suggested ending, ask *Why do you think that?* (Or, for children who cannot yet cope with 'why' questions: *What makes you think that?*) Responses which relate to the content of the story are to be especially encouraged.

Writing
Children to write and illustrate an ending for the story. This could be done individually or in pairs, and some children should use a word-processing package (e.g. Pendown), if possible.

(Technology link)

Retelling a story
Return to the story another time. Before reading, can children tell what happened in the story in the book without looking at it.

Shared reading
Now that the story is familiar, children should be able to cope with the reading independently. Guide them to picture cues, context cues, initial letters or blends, etc.

Reading their own work
Children can now share the reading of the story in the book and take turns to read their own endings.

Predicting endings
Worksheet 2b

2b

Work with small groups. Read the title of the worksheet.
Section A: help the children read the sentences for pictures 1 and 2. Help them choose a final picture, and discuss reasons for their choice. If possible, they should write their own sentences on line 3 to go with their chosen picture. (If pupils are unable to write independently, the teacher should ask them to compose two sentences, one for each of the alternative pictures. Write these down, and let pupils choose which to copy on line 3.)
Section B: same procedure, but after discussing the pictures the pupil should draw his/her own predicted ending and write a sentence to describe it.

(Technology link)

(page 5)

Then she saw spiders, a dragon, and a witch.

?????

Discussion
Further possible follow-up: general discussion relating the story to the pupil's own experience, e.g. *Does anyone watch football in your house? Do you argue about who should watch the TV? Do you ever stare at clouds and see pictures? What sort of things?*
Discussion about imagining things: *Claire imagined the things in the sky – what other things do people imagine?* (e.g. monsters in shadows at night, pictures in the fire, imaginary friends, pretend games).

Imagining and writing
Children can draw a picture of something they have imagined (e.g. a monster, my imaginary friend, me as a princess). After discussing it with the teacher or a friend, they can write a few explanatory sentences underneath.
Some children should use Pendown, or other word-processing package, if possible.

Poem and inference
The following riddle-poem has a strong rhyme and rhythm and is suitable for learning by heart, one line at a time. Watch out for the children who have more than average difficulty: they may need extra help to develop phonological awareness.

Science links: forces, wind.

White sheep, white sheep, on a blue hill,
When the wind stops, you all stand still.
When the wind blows, you walk away slow –
White sheep, white sheep, where do you go?

(Christina Rossetti)

Technology link

What are the white sheep? What is the blue hill?

Science link: characteristics of materials

The poem also makes a good centrepiece for a cloud collage. Pupils could choose appropriate fabric/material to represent clouds.

Books
Picture books:
Clouds, Peggy Blakeley (A & C Black)
Lonely Cloud, Boswell Taylor (Hodder & Stoughton)
Story (for pupils nearing Level 2 to read themselves):
'Clouds' in *Mouse Tales,* Arnold Lobel (Puffin I Can Read)
Read aloud story:
'Annabelle and the Cloud' from *Time and Again Stories,* Donald Bissett (Young Puffin)

Holiday shopping (pages 6 – 7)

Lists/Environmental print/Discussion

First picture:
What does the girl need?
Where might she be going on holiday?
Why have they made a list?
Which sort of shop will they go to?

> Science/Geography link: variations in climate

Picture of store:
Discuss environmental print. Can the children read/guess what all the signs say?
Discuss and explain as necessary.
Where will the girl get all the things she needs?

Final picture:
Do the children know what a receipt is? *What is dad looking at? Why is he looking like that? Have they bought everything on their list?*
Match the handwritten words to the printed words on the till receipt. (Perhaps bring in some receipts.)

Role-play/Environmental print

Create a 'big store' in the classroom with pay desk, lift, etc. Make bright signs and labels for everything (as in illustration). The store could be associated with clothes for hot weather or winter holidays (or both). Children take roles – cashier, shop assistants, shoppers (mums/dads/children). Make shopping lists, receipts, etc.

> Technology link

Discussion/Personal writing

Have you been shopping in a big store? What do you remember about it? Do you like shopping for clothes? What's good/bad about it?

Writing/Story structure

Children write about an occasion when they went shopping for clothes. Beginning: say what you wanted to buy and where you went.
Middle/end: about the shops and what happened.
Some pupils should use Pendown or other word-processing package, if possible.

> Technology link

Matching handwriting and print/Writing
Worksheet 2c

Section A: pupils match items on receipts to those on list, as shown.
Section B: pupils write the shopping list to go with the shopping, then match items to words as shown. (For 'beginners' pupils, the teacher may display a selection of familiar holiday shopping words, from which they can choose the ones they need.)

2c

Books

New Clothes for Mary, Mary Dickinson (Hippo)
Raymond Rabbit Goes Shopping, Lynne Dennis (Picturemac)
Teddybears Go Shopping, Susanna Gretz (Hippo)
The Shopping Basket, John Burningham (Picture Lions)
Going Shopping, Celia Berridge (Kingfisher)

Discussion: the seasons

The question of summer and winter holidays and appropriate clothes provides an opening for discussion of the seasons of the year.
Do children know the seasons and their sequence?

(Science link: seasonal changes)

What sort of things happen in spring/summer/autumn/winter? Which season do they like best? etc.

Song
(To the tune of 'John Brown's Body')

> I wear my silk pyjamas in the summer
>   when it's hot,
> I wear my flannel night-shirt in the winter
>   when it's not,
> And sometimes in the autumn when the
>   leaves begin to fall
> I slip between the sheets with nothing
>   on at all!
>
> Oh, I was only only foolin',
> I was only only foolin',
> I was only only foolin'
> 'Bout when the leaves begin to fall!

Worksheet 2d: Categorisation
Discuss the pictures/seasons. Pupils then write the names of the items around the page in the appropriate clouds.

2d

(Science link: night/day in seasonal changes)

Poem
'Bed in Summer'

> In winter I get up at night
> And dress by yellow candlelight.
> In summer, quite the other way,
> I have to go to bed by day.
>
> I have to go to bed and see
> The birds still hopping on the tree,
> Or hear the grown-up people's feet
> Still going past me on the street.
>
> And does it not seem hard to you,
> When all the sky is clear and blue
> And I should like so much to play,
> To have to go to bed by day?
>
> (Robert Louis Stevenson)

Books
Picture books:
Spring, Summer, Autumn, Winter, all by Colin McNaughton (Walker Books) – these are board books for younger children, but they have amusing pictures which give plenty of discussion material and brief captions.

Stories for pupils nearing Level 2 to read themselves:
Frog and Toad All Year, Arnold Lobel (Puffin I Can Read)

Sun out – rain in

(page 8)

(Readability: Level 1+
Most children approaching Level 2 should be able to read this with minimal help.)

Discussion

Discuss the events in the picture, relating them to children's own experience, e.g. *What do you feel like when it's rainy and you can't go out? What do you like to do outside? How can you tell when it's going to rain?*
(See also: 'Rain-banishing rhymes' in Book 1 (pages 12 – 13), and A A Milne's poem 'Waiting at the Window' in *Now We Are Six,* Puffin.)

Factual content of story

What is happening in the 'drying out' picture? Where is the water from the washing/puddle going?
Draw attention to the cyclical nature of the story, e.g. *Have you noticed anything about the first and last pictures?*
This can lead to discussion of the water cycle, which is simply illustrated in the story (see below).

> Science link: heat and change

Fiction/Non-fiction

Explain that some books (or parts of books) tell invented stories – fiction – while some give facts and information – non-fiction. Can the children identify fiction/non-fiction books in the class library?

Worksheet 2e
This worksheet provides a follow-up for this.

Discussion: the water cycle

Mention other familiar cycles (e.g. days of the week, the seasons). *What do you think 'cycle' means? Can you think of other things which happen in cycles? Can you explain what happens in the water cycle?* (Keep this simple)

> Science link: patterns of weather, etc.

(page 9)

Writing sentences

Help the group to expand the first caption ('looking out') into a complete sentence to explain what is happening in the picture (e.g. 'The boy and his mum are looking out of the window'). Write the sentence on the board, stressing correct punctuation. Ask the group to supply sentences for the other captions on page 8 in the same way, and write these up too.

This activity provides an opportunity for talking about language.

In each case, the caption consists of the 'doing word'. (You could call it a 'verb' if you prefer but don't expect the children to remember!) The pupils must decide who/what is doing it and any other information necessary to make the sentence make sense. After practising together on six sentences, pupils can be asked to create their own sentences for the five pictures on page 9, building them around the 'doing words'. This could be done individually or in pairs, and some pupils should use Pendown or other word processing package, if possible. Assess for content and punctuation.

Action rhyme

'Incy Wincy spider' (see notes to Book 1, page 13).

Song

The hymn 'Glad That I Live Am I' is found in many collections of hymns for primary schools. It provides another perspective on the water cycle.

Books

Picture books:
The Bears Who Stayed Indoors, Susannah Gretz (Picture Puffin)
See also books listed for Book 1, page 12.
Story which pupils nearing Level 2 can read by themselves:
'The Corner' in *Frog and Toad All Year,* Arnold Lobel (Puffin I Can Read)

What shall I wear today? *(page 10)*

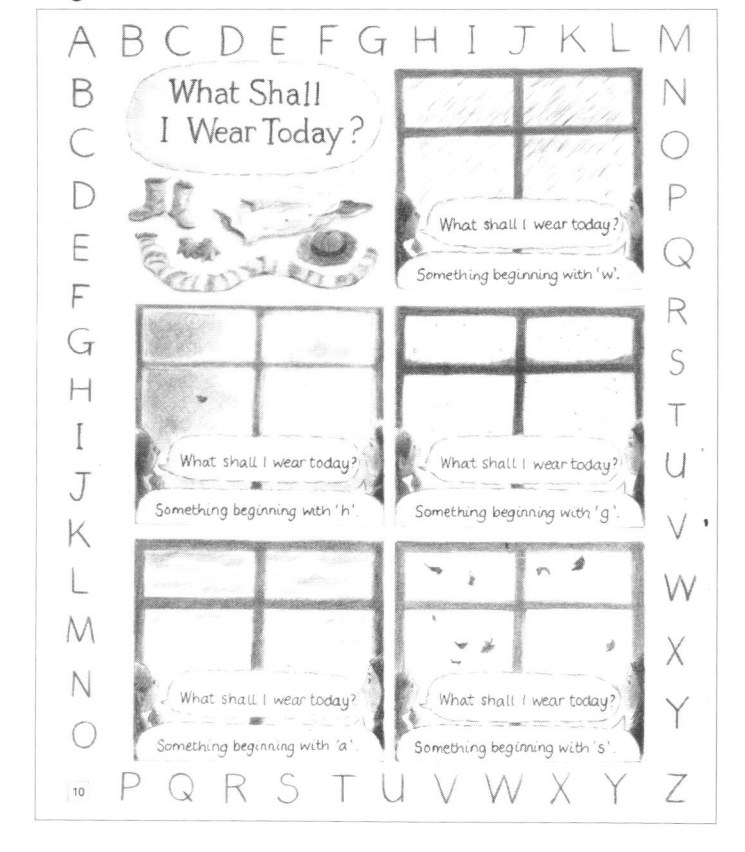

Alphabet

Discuss alphabet and practise, if necessary. A popular tune for singing the alphabet is given below.

Watch out for children who have particular difficulty with learning the alphabet – this can be an early indicator of problems in auditory memory and/or the sequencing of information, which can affect reading progress.

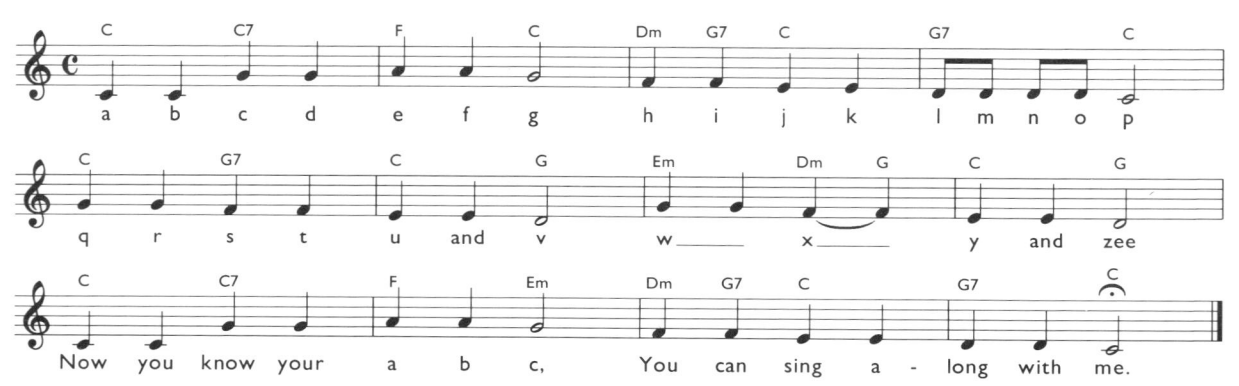

Reading/Initial letter sounds

Read the speech bubbles in the first frame to the children. Thereafter, they should be able to read them themselves. Let them guess the answers (there are picture clues, if necessary).

Discussion

Clothing appropriate to various weathers: *What sort of clothes do you need in sunny/rainy/cold weather?* etc. *What sort of material are clothes for sunny/rainy/cold weather made of?* etc. *What qualities do these materials have?* etc.

Science links: heat and cold; characteristics of materials.

Poems

A A Milne's 'John Had Great Big Waterproof Boots On' in *When We Were Very Young* and 'Furry Bear' in *Now We Are Six* would be appropriate here.

Initial letters/Blends

String up a washing line on which children can peg cut-out items of clothing labelled with their initial letters (e.g. h for hat, s for sock, n for nightie, etc.) using clothes pegs. (Later, the washing line can be used for initial blends, e.g. trousers, dress, shirt, sweater, gloves, stocking.)

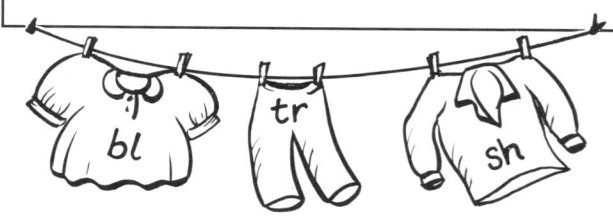

The school outing *(page 11)*

Discussion/Inference/Reading
What's happening in this picture?
Let pupils use picture context/their own reading skills to work out what is going on. Read them the note from school, if necessary.
What magazine do you think the boy is holding? Why has he got it? What is he watching on TV and why? What is the weather going to be like? What clothes will he need? What footwear (why 'footwear')? Anything else? (waterproof bag for lunch?)
NB Activities and material relating to weather forecasting are included with the notes to the Weather Rhymes on the back cover of Book 2.

> Science links: information technology; predicting weather; characteristics of materials.

Words and symbols/Environmental print
Apart from the magazine and the note, are there any other words in the picture?
Instruction panel on video machine:
What are the words on a video machine, and what do they mean?
Information is given in the picture in another way than words – *How? What symbols can you find and what do they mean?* (Weather symbols, fast forward and rewind symbols, 3 for TV channel.)
What other symbols do you know? (e.g. washing instructions, road signs, no smoking, etc.)

Discussion and writing: outings
Talk about children's own experience of school trips and other outings, and especially how they were affected by the weather. This provides a possible writing opportunity, although an immediate account of a genuine outing would be preferable.

Books
Picture books:
Mr Gumpy's Outing, John Burningham (Cape)
Wilberforce Goes on a Picnic, Margaret Gordon (Picture Puffin)
Read aloud story:
'A Class Trip' from *Tales from Allotment Lane School,* Margaret Joy (Puffin)

One foggy day (page 12)

Alphabet

For this rhyme we have used the alphabet names, as opposed to letter sounds.

Keep an eye open for those children who are still unsure of the connection between names and sounds, and need further clarification. Be ready also for many children to have difficulty with the letters W, U and Y, where letter names and letter sounds are extremely confusing. Some time spent clarifying this (through games and play activities) in the early stages can be very helpful.

Worksheet 2f | 2f
This worksheet provides practice in ordering the alphabet.

Reading/Discussion

Read the rhyme and guess the shapes. Discuss fog/mist. *Have you ever been in a fog/mist? What's it like? Why can it be dangerous? Do you know what causes it?* etc.

Science link: effects of weather

One foggy day,
All fuzzy and grey,
I saw a shape beginning with A,
I looked and looked and it was an . . .

One foggy day,
All fuzzy and grey,
I saw a shape beginning with B,
I looked and looked and it was a . . .

One foggy day,
All fuzzy and grey,
I saw a shape beginning with C,
I looked and looked and it was a . . .

Alphabet sound

Can anyone work out how we carry on this rhyme? (Give hints until most children have got it.)
What might I see next?

Foggy day game

Play the game, going round the group. The entire group chants the rhyme, supplying the appropriate letter. Children take it in turns to supply an item beginning with the particular letter of the alphabet they have reached.

Alphabet sound/Memory training

After they have played the game a few times, you may introduce the refinement of remembering what has gone before, e.g...
I saw shapes beginning with A, B, C, D, E. I looked and looked and saw an apple, a bike, a clock, a dog and an elephant. As well as helping pupils to learn the alphabet, this is a useful exercise for developing auditory memory skills.

Books

Picture book:
Mog in the Fog, Jan Pienkowski (Picture Puffin)

Read aloud stories:
'The Foggy Shopping' from *Secrets and Other Stories,* Joan Wyatt (Puffin)
Postman Pat's Foggy Day, John Cunliffe (Hippo)

Brrrr! *(page 13)*

Poetry/Reading
Read the poems, and then let children help with the reading (as in notes for 'All sorts', page 2).

Discussion/Sounds/Language

'Ice'
Have you seen ice? Walked on icy puddles/grass? Try saying the final two lines together, emphasising the 'Crrrr'.
Which letters say the Crrrr sound? Do we usually put lots of r's together? Why has the poet done it here? Can you see another word on the page where there are many r's? (Brrrr!) *How would you read that? What does it mean?*
Point out that these are not real words but a writer trying to show sounds with letters.
(Note also Grrrr for an angry dog and Prrrr for a happy cat.)

> Science links: heat and cold; condensation; effects of weather on environment and the human body.

'Dragon Smoke'
Have you ever noticed your breath in the air? In what sort of weather does it happen? Do you know why?
This poet uses letters to show a sound too – can the pupils identify it? (Huff)
What sort of sounds does the wind make? Can you use letters to show these sounds?
Help pupils to experiment in building sounds with letters.
What about the rain/snow?

> Science link: characteristics of sounds

ICE
When it is the winter time
I run up the street
And I make the ice laugh
With my little feet
Crickle crackle crickle
Crrreeet crrreeet crrreeet.

Dorothy Aldis

Dragon Smoke
Breathe and blow
white clouds
   with every puff.
It's cold today,
   cold enough
to see your breath.
Huff!
   Breathe dragon smoke today!

Lilian Moore

Jack Frost
Watch out, watch out
Jack Frost's about –
He's after your fingers and toes,
And all through the night
This gay little sprite
Is working where nobody knows.

Books
Picture books:
See books listed for pages 7, 8 and 10 of Big Book 1.
Stories which pupils nearing Level 2 could read for themselves:
'Down the Hill' from *Frog and Toad All Year*, Arnold Lobel (Puffin I Can Read)
'What Will Little Bear Wear?' from *Little Bear*, Elsie Holmelund Minarick (Puffin I Can Read)

'Jack Frost'
Because of lack of space we did not include verses 2 and 3 in the pupil's book:

He'll climb each tree.
So nimble is he,
His silvery powder he'll shake;
To windows he'll creep.
And while we're asleep.
Such wonderful pictures he'll make.

Across the grass
He'll merrily pass,
And change all its greenness to white;
Then home he will go.
And laugh, 'Ho! ho! ho!
What fun I have had in the night!'

Have you seen frost patterns on windows, grass, etc.? Where do they come from?
Pupils could try making Jack Frost patterns on a window. Melt washing soda crystals in hot water. Wipe the solution with a sponge into a pattern on the window. As the water evaporates, crystal patterns will be left.

> Science links: water/solutions; heat and cold.

Making a snowstorm *(page 14)*

Preparation
Most children should be able to provide a few plastic figures (Indians, soldiers, trees, animals, etc. from crackers and party bags, or cake decorations) for their own snowstorm scenes. The follow-up work for this activity is more fun if a few figures can be included in each tableau.
Silver glitter added to the white plastic cuttings gives a more exotic effect.

Reading/Following instructions
Read the instructions with the children, making sure they understand the importance of the sequence. Pupils should be able to make their own snowstorms, with a little teacher supervision.

Technology link

Discussion/Writing
In small groups, discuss the characters in each child's snowstorm, imagining a background for each one. *Who are they? What are their names? Where are they? Why are they there?*
Children can then write stories about their own characters. *How does your story start? What happens to your character (s)?*

Sequencing/Context cueing
Worksheet 2g: concept keyboard
This worksheet is an A4 overlay for a concept keyboard. If another size is required, it could be enlarged or reduced on a photocopier. Make grid planner as shown here.

Science link: information technology

Work with a small group.
The pictures on the overlay are in the wrong order. Pupils guess which should be first, and press picture. Numbered sentence will appear on screen. When they find correct sentence, help them to read it. Pupils thus build up instructions for making a raingauge.

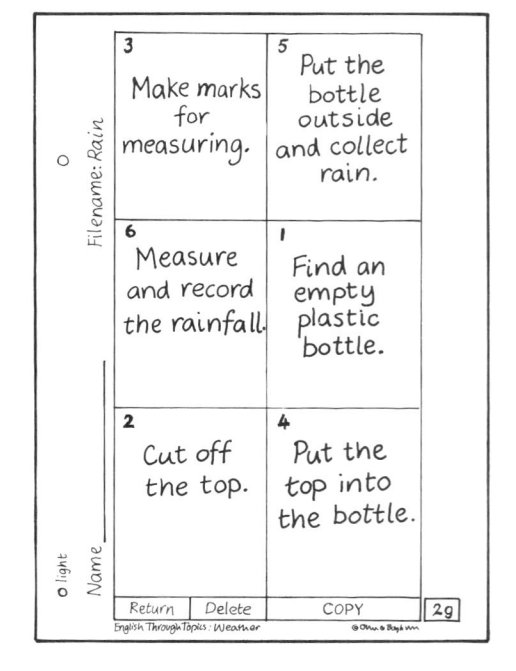

Sequencing instructions/Following written instructions
Each pupil (or pair of pupils) should have a worksheet and a print-out from the concept keyboard. They should cut out the pictures and sentences, match them, and mount/paste them in order on another sheet. If possible, they should then use the instructions to make a raingauge.

(page 15)

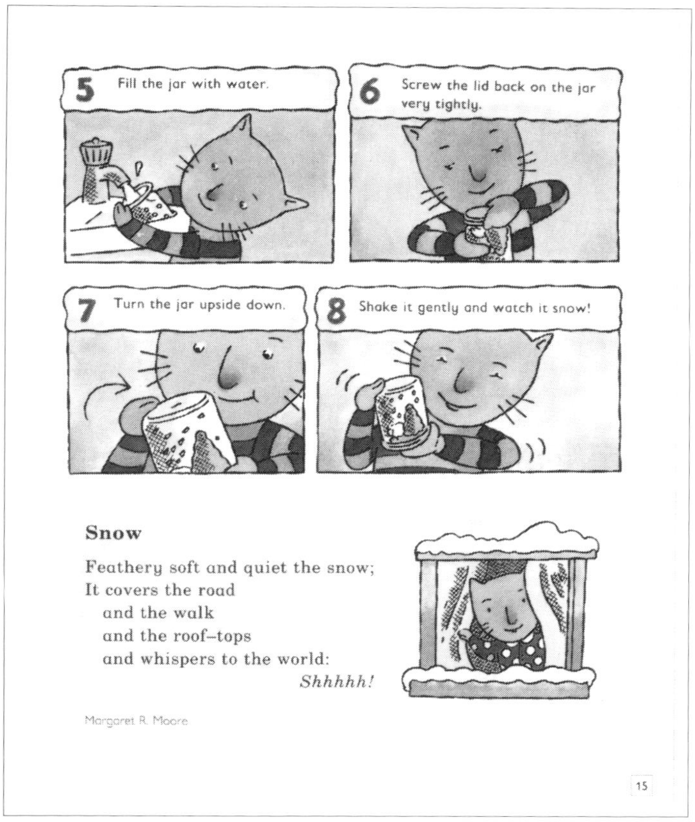

> 5. Fill the jar with water.
> 6. Screw the lid back on the jar very tightly.
> 7. Turn the jar upside down.
> 8. Shake it gently and watch it snow!
>
> **Snow**
>
> Feathery soft and quiet the snow;
> It covers the road
>   and the walk
>   and the roof–tops
>   and whispers to the world:
>   Shhhhh!
>
> Margaret R. Moore

Poem

Science links: melting snow; change; colour and light.

The following poem was not included in the Pupil's Book because of lack of space, but it is a memorable one, and provides scope for much discussion:

> Water has no colour.
> Snow is purest white.
>   I wonder where
>   The white all went
>   From the melting snow
>   Last night.
>
>   (Ilo Orleans)

Well, where did it go?!

Books

Picture books:
The Big Snowstorm, Hans Petersen (Burke, 1974)
Nip of Winter, Peggy Blakeley (A & C Black)
Read aloud story:
'You Never Know' from *Matthew's Secret Surprises,* Teresa Verschoyle (Young Puffin)

Reading/Discussion/Sounds

'Snow'
Discuss relating to the children's own experience.
This is a very quiet poem. What words in the poem tell us that we should say it quietly? (quiet, whispers, shhh)
Shhhhh! is another example of letters being used to show a sound. Can pupils remember (and write?) some of the sounds represented in the Brrrr! poems?
Why does the poet think snow is a quiet weather? How does it make the world quiet?

Science links: effects of weather on the environment; heat and cold.

The poem is an example of non-rhyming verse. The way it is set out shows how it should be read. Demonstrate with exaggerated pronunciation and a finger under the words. Pupils could then try whispering the poem in unison. Or it could be split up, line by line, to be whispered by individual/paired voices, with everyone joining in for the final 'Shhh!'
This is an opportunity to look at the 'sh' blend. Pupils could collect words beginning (and ending?) with 'sh'.

The wind who wanted to play (pages 16 – 17)

The Wind Who Wanted To Play

People in the play:
Storyteller 1   Storyteller 2
The Wind   A girl
A man   A woman
A boy   A mother

Storyteller 1 One day, the wind woke up from a little nap and said . . .

Wind I feel like playing today. I will go to the town and find people to play with. I will make them happy.

Storyteller The wind blew away to the town. Soon he saw a little girl walking to school with her new umbrella.

Wind That little girl looks fed up. I'll play with her and make her happy.

Storyteller 1 The wind blew around the little girl. It blew her new umbrella inside out.

Little Girl Oh no! My new umbrella is broken. Bother that wind!

All Wind, wind, go away! This is not the place to play!

Storyteller 2 The wind saw that the little girl was not happy so he blew on.

Storyteller 1 Then the wind saw a man walking down the road, wearing a hat.

Wind That man looks fed up. I'll play with him and make him happy.

Storyteller 2 The wind blew around the man. It blew off his hat.

Man Oh no! My hat has blown away. Bother that wind!

All Wind, wind, go away! This is not the place to play.

Storyteller 1 The wind saw that the man was not happy, so he blew on.

Storyteller 2 Next he saw a woman putting out her dustbin.

Wind That woman looks fed up. I'll play with her and make her happy.

Storyteller 1 The wind blew around the woman. It blew the lid off the dustbin. Rubbish went everywhere.

Woman Oh no! Look at all the rubbish. Bother that wind!

All Wind, wind, go away. This is not the place to play!

Storyteller 2 The wind saw that the woman was not happy, so he blew on.

(Reading levels:
Storyteller 1 – Level 2
Storyteller 2 – Level 2
The wind   – Level 2
A girl   – Level 2
A boy   – Level 1+
A man   – Level 1+
A woman   – Level 1+
A boy   – Level 1+
A mother   – Level 1+
The play is provided as reading practice and the basis of collaborative work for small groups of children. It should be tackled in three stages.)

Stage 1: Reading/Discussion

The children should hear the whole play while following in their books. Teacher should read both Storyteller parts, while competent readers take the other parts, and whole group joins in with the choruses.
Talk about the characters and the way the script is laid out. Point out the repetition in the dialogue.

Stage 2: Group reading

Groups of nine children can then read the play for themselves. The more competent readers should take the Storytellers parts. Before reading, discuss the script again: *How do you know when to speak?* etc. (See 'Punctuation' notes.)
They will probably require help to read the play through the first time, but should be allowed to try for themselves thereafter.

Punctuation

Once the children are familiar with the text, play-reading provides an excellent opportunity to focus attention on punctuation. Check that children recognise each punctuation mark, and know its function and the effect it should have on their reading.

full stop – to show the end of a sentence (pause before reading on)
comma – to show a short break in a sentence (no need to pause)
exclamation mark – a special full stop that shows a raised voice (say the words before it in a louder voice)
question mark – a special full stop that shows you are asking a question (say the words before it in a questioning voice).
For example, for each punctuation mark:
Can you find one of these? What does it tell you to do? How would it help you to read that bit of the play? Can you find any more?

(pages 18 – 19)

> **Storyteller 1** At the edge of the town, the wind saw a boy and his mother in their garden.
> **Wind** They look fed up. I'll play with them and make them happy.
> **Storyteller 2** The wind blew around the mother and made her washing flap.
> **Mother** Oh good! The wind has come to play. Now my washing will dry.
>
> **Storyteller 1** The wind blew around the boy and lifted his kite into the air.
> **Boy** Oh good! The wind has come to play. Now my kite will fly.
> **Storyteller 2** The wind saw that the boy and his mother were happy.
> **Wind** Hurray! At last I have found someone to play with. I have made these people happy.
> **All** Wind, wind, you can stay. You have found a place to play.

Stage 3: various options

Group work/Mime
Two groups could work together – one group reading the play, while their counterparts in the other group (minus the Storytellers, who will have to join the chorus) act it out, miming the events.

Group work/Taped presentation
Groups could record the play on tape, with percussion introduction and sound effects. This activity would require previous discussion and rehearsal under teacher supervision, e.g. *When should the wind make blowing noises? How can we make the sound of a breaking umbrella/toppling rubbish/sheets flapping in the wind?*
An adult would be necessary to supervise and organise the actual taping of the play.

(Technology link)

Group work/Puppetry
Another method of presentation is as a puppet show. This involves the design and production of simple puppets (e.g. stick puppets/sock puppets for the human characters, a stick with swirling paper streamers for the wind). Nine children could then read the play, while others manipulate the puppets appropriately.

(Technology link)

Information Technology
Some types of production may be suitable for an audience from another class, or even parents (asked to turn up a few minutes earlier than usual to collect children from school). In this case, a programme could be planned, giving details of performers, puppeteers, costume/set designers, etc. This could be produced using Pendown or other simple desktop publishing/word-processing techniques.

Poem/Drama

Using maximum space available, pupils can mime the actions suggested by this poem.

> Science links: observation of materials; similarities and differences.

A windy day

    Round and round the washing line goes –
    over and over twist all the clothes.
    Sometimes they're fat and sometimes thin
    as the wind comes out, then blows back in.

    Round and over and in and out,
    the wind is blowing things about.

    The wind blows here, the wind blows there,
    making fallen leaves dance everywhere.
    Down on the ground, then up in the sky.
    Some twirling low and then whirling high.

    Round and over and in and out,
    the wind is blowing things about.

    Children have fun and children chase
    as the wild wind blows from place to place.
    It tickles faces and tangles hair,
    but neither the wind nor the children care.

    Round and over and in and out,
    the wind is blowing things about.

              (Linda Hammond)

Worksheet 2h: sentence punctuation

Each section consists of several short passages from stories given in the Pupil's Book or Teacher's Notes (page 66). Each passage must be split up into sentences by the addition of full stops and capital letters. The sections are not intended to be completed in a single session.

Rhyme/Following instructions

This old song about the wind accompanies an action game useful for practising 'right' and 'left', and sequencing actions:

Chorus
    Stir up the pudding oh!
    Diddle diddle doh
    Stir up the pudding oh!
    The March Winds blow.

    Put your right leg in,
    Put it to the ground,
    Put your hands upon your head,
    And turn around.

Chorus
    Put your left leg in, etc.
Chorus
    Put your right hand in, etc.
Chorus
    Put your left hand in, etc.
Chorus
    Put your right ear in, etc.
Chorus
    Put your left ear in, etc.
Chorus
    Put your whole self in, etc.
Chorus

Books

Picture books:
See books listed for Book 1, page 6.

Story which pupils nearing Level 2 should be able to read for themselves:
'The Mouse And The Winds' from *Mouse Tales,* Arnold Lobel (Puffin I Can Read)

Read aloud stories:
'The Two Little Men and the Toad and Billy Wind', Andrew Wilkinson, from *Listen With Mother Stories,* ed. Dorothy Edwards (Young Lion)
'What The Wind Brought' from *Matthew's Secret Surprises,* Teresa Verschoyle (Young Puffin)

Poem

See also A A Milne's poem 'Wind on the Hill' in *Now We Are Six* (Methuen)

Kite display

(page 20)

Discussion/Environmental print
What's this poster about?
What do you know about kites? etc.
Information in the poster:
(help the children to read any words they ask for.)
Which word says 'kite'? How many can you count?
(Do some count 'kit'? Can they see the difference?)
When is the display? (Day? Date?)
Where is it? What does 'weather permitting' mean?
How much does it cost? What sort of thing will be happening?

Writing/Design
After discussion of what information should be included (what? when? where? how much?), pupils could design and make tickets for the kite display. Perhaps some could use a word-processor.

Poem
This poem makes a good centre piece for a collage of decorated kites:

> I often sit and wish that I
> Could be a kite up in the sky.
> I'd ride upon the breeze and go
> Whichever way the wild winds blow.

Song
Many pupils will probably be familiar with the song 'Let's Go Fly A Kite' on the Disney video *Mary Poppins*.

Books
Picture book:
The Carnival Kite, Grace Hallworthy (Methuen)

Story which pupils nearing Level 2 could read for themselves:
'The Kite' from *Days With Frog and Toad,* Arnold Lobel (Puffin I Can Read)

Group work: making kites
- Discussion/Planning
  Provide a variety of materials, and encourage children to design/create their own kites.
- Reading/Following instructions
  If their own kites don't work (they are notoriously awkward things to make), this gives an excellent reason for consulting a book on the subject, e.g. *Kites To Make And Fly* (Practical Puffin)

Technology link

Science link: characteristics of materials

Rain *(page 21)*

Poetry/Reading
Read the poems for fun, encouraging children to join in. All are suitable for rhythmic chanting and learning by heart. As the rhythms are strong, they are also suitable for accompaniment by the rhythmic drumming of fingertips on desks to represent the sound of rain.

Letter sounds: rainy words
After reading the poems again, look at the way in which the sounds of rain have been represented in the picture (cf. Brrr poems and Shh for snow). Can the pupils decode the various rainy words in the illustration from their sounds?
Notice the difference between 'pit' and 'pat'/'splish' and 'splosh' – this could be used as an introduction to the concept of vowels.
Try making the different rain sounds – using voices, drumming with fingers, dripping water into a bowl. Look at the letters and letter blends used in the words. (In 'splish splosh' sh again at the end, and a three-letter blend 'spl' at the beginning.)
Think of other sounds evocative of rain (plip, plop/drip, drop/splat/splash, etc.) and ask children to encode them with letters.

Science link: types of sound

See also 'Rain' pages in Book 1, pages 12 – 14.

Group work/Planning
Representing rain in different ways, e.g. musically (pupils make up rain sequences on various percussion instruments, and tape a selection of their favourites); visually (splatter paintings/flicking and dripping coloured paint); verbally (encoding sounds as described above). These representations could be combined in a 'multi-media display'.

Science link: sounds/music

2i *Worksheet 2i:* **phonological awareness**
Either: ask children to invent words, using letter sounds, to represent each of the sounds illustrated in the picture.
Or: write a selection of onomatopoeic words on the blackboard from which they can choose the most appropriate ones to fill in the spaces.

Books
Picture books:
A story about Kenya, where the rain is welcome – *Bringing The Rain To Kapiti Plain*, V Aardama (Macmillan)

Read aloud stories:
'The Flood' from *Ten Tales of Shellover*, Ruth Ainsworth (Young Puffin)
'A Necklace of Raindrops' from *A Necklace of Raindrops and Other Stories*, Joan Aitken (Puffin)

Guess what's outside (page 22)

(Reading level: Level 2)

Reading/Discussion

Read the story with a group of children, discussing it as necessary.
Do they know the story of Noah? (Genesis, Chapters 6 – 8)*
Are they familiar with the convention of speech bubbles and thought bubbles?

Science link: powerful effects of weather

Reading/Punctuation

Children can then help in re-reading the story. Guide them to context cues, picture cues, and initial letters/blends where necessary. Once they are familiar with the story, children who have begun to appreciate basic sentence punctuation, might try this game:

Stop – Go sentences

Pupils read the story aloud in chorus, stopping completely every time they reach a full stop or question mark. They are not allowed to continue until the teacher says 'Go!' Anyone who carries on reading after a full stop or before being given the go-ahead is out. (The game can then be played with other familiar texts.)

Group work/Discussion/Planning

The story provides scope for a lot of puppet making. Children could work in pairs, choosing creatures to represent: cats, polar bears, birds, cows, ducks. (Further animals may be added, and the story extended to include them. Pupils should suggest what extra animals would hope Mr Noah has seen outside, e.g. dogs – bones; squirrels – nuts; butterflies – flowers). The puppets need be no more complicated than painted cut-outs mounted on sticks, although pupils may have more sophisticated ideas. Similarly, the puppet theatre could be simply a table covered with a cloth, behind which various puppeteers could crawl, holding up their puppets as they recite their lines. Again, discussion and initiative may result in more polished presentation.

Technology link

Science link: animal needs

Writing/Information/Technology

If the puppet show is to be presented to another class or group, posters, tickets and programmes could be produced, using Pendown or other simple desk-top publishing programs.

Technology link

* See list of books on page 64 of these notes.

(page 23)

Songs

The following songs are two of many about Noah's Ark:

The animals went in two by two
(Traditional children's rhyme, sung to the tune of 'When Johnny Comes Marching Home')

The animals went in two by two,
Hurrah hurrah
The animals went in two by two,
Hurrah hurrah
The animals went in two by two,
The elephant and the kangaroo,
And they all went into the ark
For to get out of the rain.

The animals went in 3 by 3, etc...
The ant, the wasp and the bumble bee...

The animals went in 4 by 4, etc...
The big hippopotamus stuck in the door...

The animals went in 5 by 5, etc...
They were eating each other to keep alive...

The animals went in 6 by 6, etc...
They locked out the monkey because of his tricks...

The animals went in 7 by 7, etc...
The little pig thought he was going to heaven...

Didn't it rain? (Traditional American)

Chorus:
Now, didn't it rain, chillun,
God's gonna 'stroy this world with water,
Now didn't it rain, my Lord,
Now didn't it rain, rain, rain.

Well, it rained 40 days and it rained 40 nights,
There wasn't no land nowhere in sight,
God sent a raven to carry the news,
He histe** his wings and away he flew.

Well, it rained 40 days and 40 nights without stopping,
Noah was glad when the rain stopped a-dropping.
God sent Noah a rainbow sign,
Says, 'No more water, but fire next time.'

(**lifted)

(page 24)

Discussion: rainbows
The Bible story explains the rainbow as God's covenant to man.
Do the children know the basic scientific explanation of rainbows?

> Science links: light and colour; observation; how and why questions; reflection.

The poem refers to the way the colours of the spectrum can sometimes be seen in a puddle. *Have you ever seen rainbow colours shining in a puddle? Do you know why it happens? Have you seen them anywhere else?* (e.g. in the edge of a mirror or other bevelled glass?)

Rhyme/Brainstorming session
Read rhyme given with Teacher's Notes for Book 1, page 2. What other things can children think of which they associate with each rainbow colour?
As they give ideas, note them down on the board. It may be better to do this over several sessions, brainstorming about a couple of colours at a time.

Poem/Display
Rearrange the ideas to create a class poem about the rainbow, which can be transferred to a rainbow display – arches of rainbow colours each with a collection of words and ideas written across them, e.g.:

> 'Red is danger, poppies, blood,
> the colour of my reading book;
> red is flaming fire, hot,
> my favourite dress, Lesley's hair;
> red is tomato sauce and red peppers
> red is bright colour.'

Worksheet 2j: Weather riddles/Reading and writing sentences
This worksheet relates to weather in general.

In the Rain
There is no colour in the rain
It's only water, wet and plain.
It makes damp spots upon my book
And splashes on my new dress, look!
But puddles, in the rainy weather,
Glisten like a peacock's feather.

— Pere Cisle

Books
Picture books:
Noah's Ark*, Jane Ray (Orchard Books)
How The Animals Saved The Ark, Roger Smith (Picture Puffin)
The Great Flood, P Spier (World's Work)
Noah's Ark, Roger McGough and Ljljana Rylands (Picture Lions)
See also notes for Big Book, page 2.

Read aloud stories:
'The Flood' from *Melanie Brown and the Jar of Sweets*, Pamela Oldfield (Faber)
'The Last Slice of Rainbow' from *The Last Slice of Rainbow and Other Stories*, Joan Aiken (Puffin)

* Using text from the Authorised Version of the Bible.

Weatherwise *(back cover)*

Discussion

Weather lore
Read the rhymes, and help children to understand the meanings.

Do they know any other rhymes/sayings about the weather? (e.g.: 'A sunshiny shower won't last half an hour.' Asking parents and grandparents may produce a crop, including local ones. See also notes to Book 3, page 4.)

(Science links: collating observations; recording findings.)

Do you think this rhyme/saying is true? Why/why not?

It might be possible to check on the accuracy of one or two of the rhymes by keeping a 'weather watch' during the project.

Weather forecasting
Look back to illustration on page 11 of Book 2. Discuss weather forecasts, relating to children's own experience.

What's the difference between the predictions of weather people on TV and those of weather rhymes?

(Science link: technology)

What sorts of methods do television weather forecasters use to find out what the weather will be like?

Try watching some weather forecasts on the school TV during the day (or preferably video some, so that you can rewind and watch sections again). Choose short, simple summaries (e.g. those on Breakfast TV broadcasts). Discuss how the bulletin is organised (e.g. morning/afternoon/longer term forecast); whereabouts on the map is relevant for the pupils; what name is given to their part of the country (e.g. 'the North West', 'the Southern Uplands'); the various symbols used; the sort of vocabulary used by weather persons.

Picture books
The Weather Cat, Helen Cresswell (Collins)
Mr Wolf's Week, Colin Hawkins (Picture Lions)

Folktales for storytelling/drama

Listening/Drama/Storytelling/Cooperative work

Using an African folktale and a story from Greek mythology:

Split the class into two groups, A and B.

With group A:

- Work where you cannot be overheard by group B members.
- Read the children the story of 'The Hen, the Frog and the Thunderstorm' (see opposite) using the picture as a focus for their attention.
- Discussion: e.g. *How was the frog lazy? What other words could you use to describe the frog?* (nasty, bullying) *What words could you use to describe the hen?* (clever, well-prepared)
- Read the story through again, with a view to dramatising it.
- Drama: pair off the children. Call each pair 1 and 2. 1 plays the hen, 2 plays the frog, and they act out the story. Swap over, and act it again.
- Tell children that they are each going to be paired with a member of group B, and they have to tell their partner the story and then act it out.
- Tell the story a final time (don't read it this time).
- Each group A child practises storytelling and organising the drama activity with a member of group B.

With group B:

- Work where you cannot be overheard by group A members.
- Read the children 'The story of Icarus' (see page 68), using the picture as a focus for their attention.
- Discussion: e.g. *Why did Icarus fall out of the sky? What is wax like?*
- Read the story again, with a view to dramatising it.
- Drama: acting out the story, in pairs. Each child should get a go at being Icarus.
- Tell the children that they are going to be paired with a member of group B, and they have to tell their partner the story and then act it out.
- Tell the story a final time (don't read it this time).
- Each group B child practises storytelling and organising the drama activity with a member of group A.

The Hen, the Frog and the Thunderstorm
A story from Africa

Once upon a time, there was a busy little hen and a lazy little frog. One day the hen looked up and saw a big black cloud far away across the sky. 'Oh dear,' she said, 'there's going to be a storm. I'd better make a hut to shelter in. Will you help me, frog?'

But the frog was sitting on a lily pad catching flies, so he wouldn't help. The hen built a little house all by herself, and then looked up at the sky. The black cloud had come closer. 'Oh dear,' she said. 'The storm is going to be a big one. I'd better make myself a bed to sleep in while it rains. Will you help me, frog?'

But the frog was still sitting on the lily pad catching flies, and he wouldn't help. The hen made herself a cosy little bed, and then looked up at the sky again. The black cloud was almost above them. 'Oh dear,' she said. 'I'd better get some food in the house to eat while the storm's on. Will you help me, frog?'

But the frog was still sitting on a lily pad catching flies, so he wouldn't help. The hen fetched some corn into the hut, and stored some pumpkins on the roof. At that moment it started to rain, so she rushed inside.

The frog sat on his lily pad for a few minutes getting very wet, then went and banged on the hen's door. 'You'd better let me come in,' he said. 'Why?' asked the hen. 'You didn't help me make the hut.' 'No,' said the frog, 'but if you don't let me in I'll call the horrible cat who gobbles up little hens, and tell her where you are.' The hen was so frightened that she let him in.

The frog looked at the comfy little bed. 'You'd better let me sleep on that bed,' he said. 'Why?' asked the hen. 'You didn't help me make the bed.' 'No,' said the frog, 'but if you don't let me sleep in it I'll call the horrible cat who gobbles up little hens, and tell her where you are.' The hen was so frightened that she let the frog sleep in her bed.

He slept all night long, while the storm raged outside. By morning, the storm was over. The frog woke up and said, 'You'd better give me some of your food.' The hen didn't bother mentioning that he hadn't helped her fetch the food, because she knew what he'd say. But she looked out of the window and saw something that looked like another cloud in the sky – a very small cloud, coming this way.

'All right,' she said. 'Go up on the roof and bring in a pumpkin for your breakfast.' The frog hopped out on the roof. He didn't bother to look up. The thing that looked like a cloud came flying past. It was a hawk. It picked up the frog in its claws and swooped off, to eat him for its breakfast. So the little hen brought in the pumpkin and cooked it, and ate it all herself. And then she looked up at the sky to see what this new day would bring.

The Story of Icarus
A story from Ancient Greece

Long ago there lived a father and son who were being kept in a country far from their home by a wicked king. The father was called Dedalus and his son was called Icarus.

Dedalus and Icarus wanted to escape and return to their own country, which was a log way across the sea, but they had no boat in which to sail away. So they stayed, trapped in the wicked king's land, feeling sad and hopeless.

However, Dedalus was a very clever man – an inventor. He thought hard about ways of escaping, and at last he had an idea. If he could make himself and Icarus a pair of wings each, they would be able to fly up in the sky. Then they could fly over the sea and back to their own country. Dedalus set to work, designing and making the wings.

He could not buy materials from the shops or he might be found out, so he and Icarus collected birds' feathers and stuck them together. They could not buy glue either, so Dedalus used drips of wax from the candles they had to light their house. When wax is warm it goes soft, so Dedalus could use it to hold the feathers in the right positions. And when the wax went cold it set hard and held the wings together.

It took a long time, but at last Dedalus had made two pairs of wings – one for himself, and one for the boy Icarus. One fine morning, they put them on, ran along the beach and launched themselves into the sky. The wings worked! The father and son flew up and away across the sea.

Icarus thought it was great fun flying about. He started doing loop-the-loops and other tricks. He soared around, and swooped backwards and forwards. Then he decided to see how high he could fly. Up, up, up he went, higher and higher in the sky.

Dedalus saw Icarus flying up towards the warm morning sun. 'No,' he shouted. 'Come back, Icarus!' But Icarus was so high by now that he didn't hear him. 'The wax, Icarus,' shouted Dedalus. 'The wax will melt in the heat from the sun!'

He was too late. As Icarus flew nearer and nearer to the hot sun, the wax that held his wings together began to melt. The wings began to fall apart. Before Icarus knew it, he had no strong wings to hold him up in the air. He began to fall down, down, down, into the sea below.

There was nothing Dedalus could do. Icarus had flown too near to the sun. Now he was drowned in the cold sea, and his father had to fly on home all alone.

> Science links: heat and change of materials; forces; how and why questions.

Weather

Sue Palmer, Avril Barton and Peter Brinton

English Through Topics

3

it rustles

and whishes

and bangs

and twangs

Book 3

Pupils working towards Level 3

Looking at the language we use

PUPIL'S BOOK 3: resource material, linked to the theme of Weather, of the following types:
- poems and rhymes
- traditional stories from fable and folk literature
- fiction in a variety of formats (play, stories)
- picture stimuli for written work
- examples of a variety of written sources of information, different print styles and handwriting, including children's work
- picture stories showing the process of:
  — drafting and editing a piece of writing
  — reading for information
- non-fiction material
- glossaries of specialist terminology related to English work.

THE TEACHER'S NOTES: accompanying the pages from the pupil's book:
- suggestions for using the resource materials to cover Level 3 English requirements. (A guide to the layout of the teacher's notes is given on page 8.)
- more poems and rhymes
- fables and folk stories for the teachers to read or retell
- titles of books for pupils (picture books, story books, anthologies of short stories) related to the theme
- titles of books which the teacher might read to pupils (we call these 'Read aloud' books).

WORKSHEETS: practice work on:
- 3a Nouns   (link to Pupil's Book 3 page 2)
- 3b Verbs   (link to page 2)
- 3c Adjectives   (link to page 4)
- 3d statements and questions   (link to page 6)
- 3e Singular or plural   (link to page 11)
- 3f Spelling (wordsearch)   (link to page 13)
- 3g Writing complete sentences/
      reading comprehension   (link to page 16)
- 3h Sentence punctuation   (link to page 16)
- 3I Using an index   (link to page 22)
- 3j Sentence connectives   (link to page 30)

Covering the English Curriculum

The material is intended to **supplement** the ongoing language work for children working towards Level 3 and link it to the theme of Weather.

Pupil's Book 3 has been designed to provide:
- stimuli for discussion, drama, and various group activities, including group presentations;
- opportunities to listen and respond to poetry, fiction, folktales and non-fiction writing;
- opportunities to use spoken language in a wide variety of ways, including relating narrative and giving and receiving complex instructions;
- opportunities to read aloud and silently from a variety of material;
- opportunities to read for a variety of purposes;
- understanding of the techniques applicable when reading for information;
- opportunities to use inference and deduction based on previous reading experience, and to employ developing knowledge of story structure in personal writing;
- stimuli for pupils' own writing, fiction and non-fiction, chronological and non-chronological;
- information about punctuation (and practice material);
- occasional links to the teaching of spelling;
- awareness of the rule-based nature of language, including the way words can be categorised by function, and the effects of tense and singularity/ plurality on word endings;
- technical vocabulary in which to discuss the above;
- understanding of the process and purpose of drafting and editing written work, and opportunities to apply this;
- opportunities to practise joined-up handwriting and careful presentation of written work;
- opportunities to use word-processing facilities.

Links between the above and Science/Technology are indicated throughout the Teacher's Notes. There are also possible links to Art, Geography, History, Information Technology, RE, Health Education, Music and Movement. It is left to the teacher to decide how far and in what ways to exploit these cross-curricular links.

N.B. Only spelling points which arise from the resource material are covered: further systematic spelling instruction will be required.

Keeping track

The Record-keeping checklist on page 71 and the Record-keeping sheets in the *Copymasters* match the National Curriculum English Attainment Targets for Level 3 with the activities suggested in these notes. The numbers used to record these correlations are the page numbers of the Pupil's Book against which activities are recommended in the Teacher's Notes.

Please see also the notes on page 11 about record-keeping.

Record-keeping checklist

Opportunities for covering Level 3 NC English Attainment Targets

See activities suggested to accompany the pages given below in Pupil's Book 3:

Speaking and Listening													
Relate a connected narrative				7	8								
Listen/question/respond to others	2	3	5	6	7	8	9	10	11	12/13	14	15	17	18/19	23	24	25	26	27	28	31
Give instructions						8		10					17						27	29	31
Follow instructions	2	4			7	8	9	10	11	12/13			16	17	20–2		24		26	27	29	31
Reading													
Read aloud from familiar stories/poems	2	3	5	6				10	11		14			17		23		25	26	27	28–30	31
Sustained silent reading				5						12/13					20–2	23				27	28–30	
Listen to stories		3		5							14			18/19						27	28–30	
Talk about setting/storyline/characters	3				7	8		10			14		17	18/19				25		27	28	
Recall significant detail	3								11		14			18/19		23	24		26	27	28	
Appreciate meanings beyond literal using inference, deduction etc	3–5							10				14	15	18/19				25		27	28	
Recognise story structure	3				7								15	18/19				25		27	28	
Devise questions to guide information search and reading															20–2	23						
Writing													
Produce pieces of writing using sentences							7	9		11	12/13			16			24	25	26		28	30
Use full stops, capital letters, question marks				6	7			9		11	12/13			16			24	25	26	27	28	
Shape chronological accounts					7			9		11	12/13						24	25			28	
Use variety of sentence construction				6	7			9		11	12/13			16				25	26		28	30
Write more detailed stories/detailed ending					7			9			12/13							25			28	
Non-chronological writing	2			6					10				17				24	25	26			
Begin to revise and redraft				6							12/13								25	26		
Check for consistent tenses/pronouns						8	9			11	12/13									26		
Become aware of language use	2	4		6		8	9			11	12/13			16						26	27	28–30
Spelling													
Simple polysyllabic words observing common letter patterns			5	6	7			9			11	12/13									28	
Regular patterns for vowel sounds/common letter strings			5	6	7			9			11	12/13									28	
Word families and relationships	2	4		6	7			9	10	11	12/13							25	26		28	
Check accuracy when redrafting				6							12/13										28	
Handwriting (joined)													
Opportunities to practise handwriting		4		6							11	12/13						25	26		28	

This checklist refers to the National Curriculum in English at the time of going to press (Autumn 1992). An updated sheet for the revised curriculum, when known, is available free to purchasing schools, from Oliver & Boyd, Longman House, Burnt Mill, Harlow, Essex CM20 2JE.

Assessing and teaching children using ETT Book 3

(See notes on assessment in General introduction, page 11 and *Copymasters*, page ix)

The resource material is pitched for teaching purposes roughly halfway between a Level 2 and a Level 3 standard. Teacher input will, of course, vary to accommodate children's needs as they progress along the developmental continuum between Levels 2 and 3.

Progress can be informally assessed by observation of a child's performance when using the resource material and carrying out activities. For example:

	Just above Level 2 (beginner)	**Between Levels 2 and 3** (midway)	**Nearing Level 3** (independent)
Spoken English	Requires supervision to carry out group work; requires repeated explanations of activities; unsure of vocabulary related to language and topic work; unsure how to express understanding of linguistic and topic-related concepts.	Some teacher support required for group activities; requires few or no repetitions of instructions; developing control of vocabulary related to language and topic work; developing confidence in expressing linguistic and topic-related concepts.	Little supervision required for group work; explanations usually grasped at first attempt; confident of vocabulary and able to talk clearly about concepts in language and topic work.
Reading	Requires considerable teacher support to read texts labelled as Level 2+; reads with little expression or attention to punctuation; requires more than one reading to recall detail accurately.	Reads texts labelled as Level 2+ with reasonable fluency, requiring little support; developing expression in reading and beginning to attend to punctuation; generally recalls detail after one reading of a text.	Reads texts labelled as Level 2+ easily, and can manage texts labelled Level 3 with some fluency; good expression and attention to punctuation; good recall of detail.
Writing	Requires considerable teacher support to complete writing tasks suggested in Teacher's Notes; simple pieces of writing with rudimentary punctuation.	Developing confidence to tackle writing tasks in Teacher's Notes with less support; stories and non-chronological writing showing evidence of structure; basic sentence punctuation developing.	Able to complete writing tasks in Teacher's Notes reasonably independently; stories and non-chronological writing demonstrate understanding of basic elements of structure; on the whole, correct punctuation of sentences.
Spelling	Requires help with polysyllabic spellings; generally phonetic spelling of unknown words; considerable teacher support to identify and correct errors in own writing.	Needs less help with common polysyllabic words; beginning to use knowledge of common letter strings and word families to spell unknown words; developing confidence in checking for errors in own writing.	Good vocabulary of common polysyllabic words; developing confidence in using knowledge of common letter strings and word families to spell unknown words; able to check and correct own errors using established classroom strategies.
Handwriting	Requires considerable support in order to produce joined-up writing.	Able to produce clear, legible joined-up writing, with some support, for final drafts.	Always able to produce clear, legible joined-up writing in final drafts.

Contents

	Page in Pupil's Book 3
Summer and Winter	2
The North Wind and the Sun	3
Questions of weather	6
Patch and the storm	7
Out in the cold	8
Snow and snowmen	10
A weather diary	11
Drafting and editing	12
The Rat King	14
Reading for information	20
Clouds	23
Clouds and rain	23
Sun and Rain/Rainy nights	24
Splash!	25
A letter from India	26
Around the year	27
What is a rainbow?	28
Weather is full of the nicest sounds	31
Glossary	32
In the Sun and Winter Days	back cover
The twelve months	Teacher's Notes only

Summer and Winter (page 2)

Reading: poem
(Readability: Level 2)

Read the poem, discuss as appropriate.

Science links: seasonal changes; inclination of sun; listing and collating foods.

Discussion/Non-chronological writing

Seasonal differences
Discuss the differences between summer and winter. Pupils in pairs list major points of difference, in columns headed SUMMER and WINTER. (See also notes to Book 2, page 6 and notes for Book 3, back page poems.)

summer and winter

When a warm dawn brings
the sun to your eyes,
blink three times –
it's time to rise.

When cold winds whistle
around your head,
pull it under the blankets
and stay in bed.

Michael Dugan

Parts of speech: introduction
An important part of pupils' language awareness is their recognition that words can be categorised by function. Words do 'different jobs' in a sentence.

Parts of speech: nouns
(See Glossary, page 32 of Book 3.)

Worksheet 3a
This introduces the concept of nouns as 'naming words' through association with labels, and familiarises pupils with the word 'noun'.
After discussion, pupils should complete worksheets individually or in pairs.

Noun hunt and posters
Pupils in groups make (draw/paint/collage from magazine cut-outs) large posters of summer and winter scenes. Give these clear titles: 'SUMMER NOUNS' and 'WINTER NOUNS'. In discussion with teacher, pupils make and stick on labels (as in worksheet 3a) for some of the nouns in the pictures, especially those with seasonal associations.

Parts of speech: verbs
(See Glossary, page 33 of Book 3.)

Worksheet 3b
This familiarises pupils with the term 'verb' and introduces the concept of a 'doing word'. After discussion, pupils should complete the worksheet individually or in pairs.

Miming summer verbs and winter verbs
Teacher and pupils list on blackboard SUMMER VERBS (anything you might do in hot weather e.g. swim, sunbathe, play, bowl, bat, drink) and WINTER VERBS (anything you might do in cold weather, e.g. shiver, sleep, ski, kick, run). Pupils take turns to mime verbs. Rest of group guesses which verbs.

See also: notes for back page poems, on page 106 of these Teacher's Notes.

The North Wind and the Sun *(page 3)*

> **The North Wind and the Sun**
>
> **Once upon a time,** the North Wind and the Sun were chatting to each other in the sky.
> "I'm a very strong wind, you know," boasted the North Wind to the Sun.
> "Are you really?" said the Sun.
> "Oh yes, I'm much stronger than you," the North Wind went on. The Sun smiled, because the North Wind was always showing off.
>
> "I don't think you are stronger than me," said the Sun.
> "I bet I am," said the North Wind.
> She pointed to the people down on earth.
> "I can make those people do anything I like," she said.
> "I bet you can't," the Sun said.
> "I bet I can," said the North Wind.
> Just then, a man came riding along the road in front of them. He was wearing a fine new cloak.
> "I bet I can blow that man's cloak right off his back," said the North Wind.
> "I bet you can't," said the Sun.

Reading a story

(Readability: Level 2+)
Pupils who have just reached Level 2 may need to hear the story read aloud before attempting to read it themselves. Others, who are approaching a Level 3 standard, should be able to read it unaided.

Recall of detail

For example:
- *In what way did the North Wind think she was better than the Sun?*
- *How did she try to prove it?*
- *What four effects of her blowing were described in the story?*
- *What four effects of the sun's shining were described in the story?*
- *How did the sun make the man take off his cloak?*

> Science links: effects of weathering on environments; heat and insulation; temperature; forces.

Discussion: story structure

- *This story can be divided into several parts – what are they?*
  (e.g. beginning; action of wind; action of sun; end)
- *Where does each part start and end?*
- *The writer repeats certain words and phrases in the middle two sections – which words/phrases, and why does she do it?*
  (e.g. 'she blew… but she didn't blow…' is used to build up the effects of the wind's action, which get gradually more destructive.)

Discussion: fables

This story is an adaptation of a fable attributed to the Greek storyteller, Aesop, who lived around 600 BC. He is said to have been a slave, who eventually received his freedom for his storytelling powers. However, many of the fables are probably from other sources – some have been discovered on Egyptian papyri of 800 – 1000 years earlier.

- *A fable is a story which makes a point, usually about how people should/should not behave. What is the point in this fable?*
- *Think of examples of times when kindness is more powerful than cruelty in everyday life.*
- *What other fables do you know?*

Parts of speech: nouns and verbs

Follow up previous work by looking for some nouns and verbs in the story.

Parts of speech: adjectives

(See Glossary, page 33 of Book 3.)

Which adjectives are used in the story to describe
- *the young man's cloak (p. 3)?* (fine, new)
- *the world (p. 5)?* (warm, happy)
- *the water (p. 5)?* (cool)
- *the North Wind (bottom p. 5)?* (angry)

What other adjectives might you use to describe the North Wind? (e.g.: boastful, proud, conceited, cruel, unkind, powerful, strong) *the Sun?* (e.g.: kind, calm, gentle, generous, modest, strong, powerful)

Worksheet 3c
Discuss and fill the 'adjective bank' in the top corner. Pupils then complete the worksheet individually or in pairs.

Group work: an adjective bank

Create an adjective bank, with adjectives on cards filed in alphabetical order. Start with the adjectives pupils have written on their worksheets, and those which have come out of discussion. Whenever a pupil comes up with a good adjective, s/he can add it to the bank. The cards can be used for games (e.g. teacher draws out 3/4 adjectives at random, pupils have to draw a 'monster' to fit them; pupils in teams draw out an adjective each, give example of something it describes, etc.)

(page 4)

The North Wind puffed up her cheeks and began to blow. She blew the hats off people's heads . . . but she didn't blow the cloak off the man's back.

She blew the leaves off all the trees . . . but she didn't blow the cloak off the man's back.

She blew so loud that she frightened all the animals.

She blew so hard that she sank the ships at sea . . . but she didn't blow the cloak off the man's back.

The harder she blew, the tighter he pulled his cloak round him, to keep himself warm in the cold north wind.

At last the North Wind stopped for a rest. "Maybe you aren't as strong as you think" said the Sun. "Huh," sniffed the North Wind, "I bet you can't do any better.'
"Very well,' said the Sun, "I'll try if you like." He began to shine gently.

Verse/Handwriting

The following weather verse is a useful aide-memoire about the types of wind from different directions, and is suitable for handwriting practice (perhaps in instalments):

> When the wind is in the North,
> The skilful fisherman goes not forth.
> When the wind is in the South,
> It blows the bait in the fish's mouth.
> When the wind is in the East,
> It's neither fit for man nor beast.
> When the wind is in the West,
> Then it's at its very best.

Science links: air; wind; forces.

(page 5)

He shone on the flowers,
so they opened up.
He shone on the birds,
so they began to sing.

He shone on the animals,
so they lay down in the
fields and went to sleep.

He shone on the people,
so they came out into the streets
and chatted to each other.

He shone and shone until all the
world was warm and happy.

The man on the horse began to feel very hot in his new cloak. When he came to a river, he thought how lovely it would be to splash and swim in the cool water. So he took off his cloak and his other clothes, and jumped into the river.

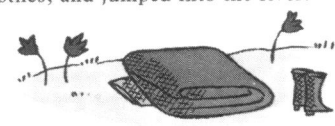

The North Wind was very angry and went into a sulk. The Sun just smiled. "There are lots of ways of being strong," he said. "I think my way is best."

Spelling links

Some spelling points which arise from words in the story:
- Irregular frequently misspelled common words with useful mnemonics:
  people (pronounce pe-o-ple, emphasising the 'o')
  horse (like 'house' but with 'r' instead of the 'u')
  clothes (made of 'cloth' with an 'e' on the end)
- Groups of words for teaching suggested by words in the story:
  wear, etc. ('Can the bear wear a pear in his ear?')
  ight words, e.g. in story, right/tight/fright + en
  oa words, e.g. in story, road, cloak, boast

Books

Picture books:
Aesop's Fables (Picturemac)
Fables, Arnold Lobel (Picturemac)
The North Wind and the Sun, Brian Wildsmith (Oxford)

Read aloud story about wind:
Mrs Pinny and the Blowing Day, Helen Morgan (Dart)
See also notes for Book 2, page 18 (books about wind) and Book 1, page 3/Book 2, page 3 (books about sun).

Discussion: folktales

When pupils are familiar with this fable, tell them the Russian folk story of 'The Frost, the Sun and the Wind':

A peasant meets the Frost, the Sun and the Wind walking along a country road, and says 'Greetings' as he passes them. The three forces of weather argue among themselves as to which one the peasant intended to greet. The Sun and Frost each claims the honour because each says he's the most powerful weather and therefore the most respected by mortals. The Wind says that they are both wrong.

Eventually they ask the peasant, who replies that he greeted the Wind. The Sun is angry and threatens to shine on the peasant and burn him. However, the Wind tells the man not to fear: he will send soft breezes to cool the sun's heat. Then the Frost threatens to freeze the peasant into a block of ice. The Wind again reassures the peasant: 'There is no frost if I blow.'

How is the wind different here from the wind in Aesop's fable? How is the sun different? Why do you think this should be? (Discussion of the climates of Greece and Russia may help here.)

Science links: heat and cold; effects of weathering on environment; response of living things to heat/cold.

Questions of weather (page 6)

(Readability: Level 2)

Reading/Poetry
Read the poems aloud with the group. 'The Sun' works well as a dialogue for two voices.

Science links: the sun; air and wind; forces – why the ships go down.

Language: questions and statements

(See Glossary, page 33 of Book 3.)
Which sentences are questions/statements in
   'The Sun'?
   'The Wind'?
What other questions could you ask about what the wind might do?
What other questions could you ask about the sun?
What is different in the way we use our voices to ask questions as opposed to making statements?
Use the poems (with exaggerated pronunciation) as illustrations.

How do we show the difference between a statement and a question in writing?

Questions of Weather

The Wind

The wind has such a rainy sound
Moaning through the town.
The sea has such a windy sound –
Will the ships go down?

The apples in the orchard
Tumble from their tree.
Oh will the ships go down, go down,
In the windy sea?

Christina Rossetti

The Sun

"Sun, Sun overhead,
What's your colour?"

"I am red."

"Sun, sun, fiery fellow,
What's your colour?"

"I am yellow."

"Sun, sun, sky of blue,
What's your colour?"

"Orange too.
I'm golden yellow,
Orange and red,
A burning fire above your head."

Robert Heidbreder

Worksheet 3d   **3d**
Gives practice in recognising and writing questions and sentences.

Language/Spelling
Adjectives made from nouns
In 'The Wind', the poet uses the adjectives 'rainy' and 'windy' – what do they describe?
These adjectives are formed from nouns – the names of sorts of weather. Many weather adjectives are formed in this way:

rain	rainy	ice	icy
cloud	cloudy	thunder	thundery
wind	windy	snow	snowy
sun	sunny	frost	frosty
fog	foggy	breeze	breezy
mist	misty		

Spelling notes
- Final -y can make an 'i' sound.
- If final -y is added, final silent -e is no longer required (as in breezy and icy).
- Note doubled consonant in sunny and foggy to retain short vowel sound.

Spelling
Note the 'wh' spelling of many 'question words' (where, why, when, which, what and – different pronunciation – who). Linking these together under the conceptual umbrella of 'question words' can help when children confuse the spellings of where/were and which/witch. If it's a 'question word' it's got a 'wh' at the beginning.

Read aloud story
'Piglet Does A Very Grand Thing' from *The House At Pooh Corner*, AA Milne (Methuen)

Patch and the storm *(page 7)*

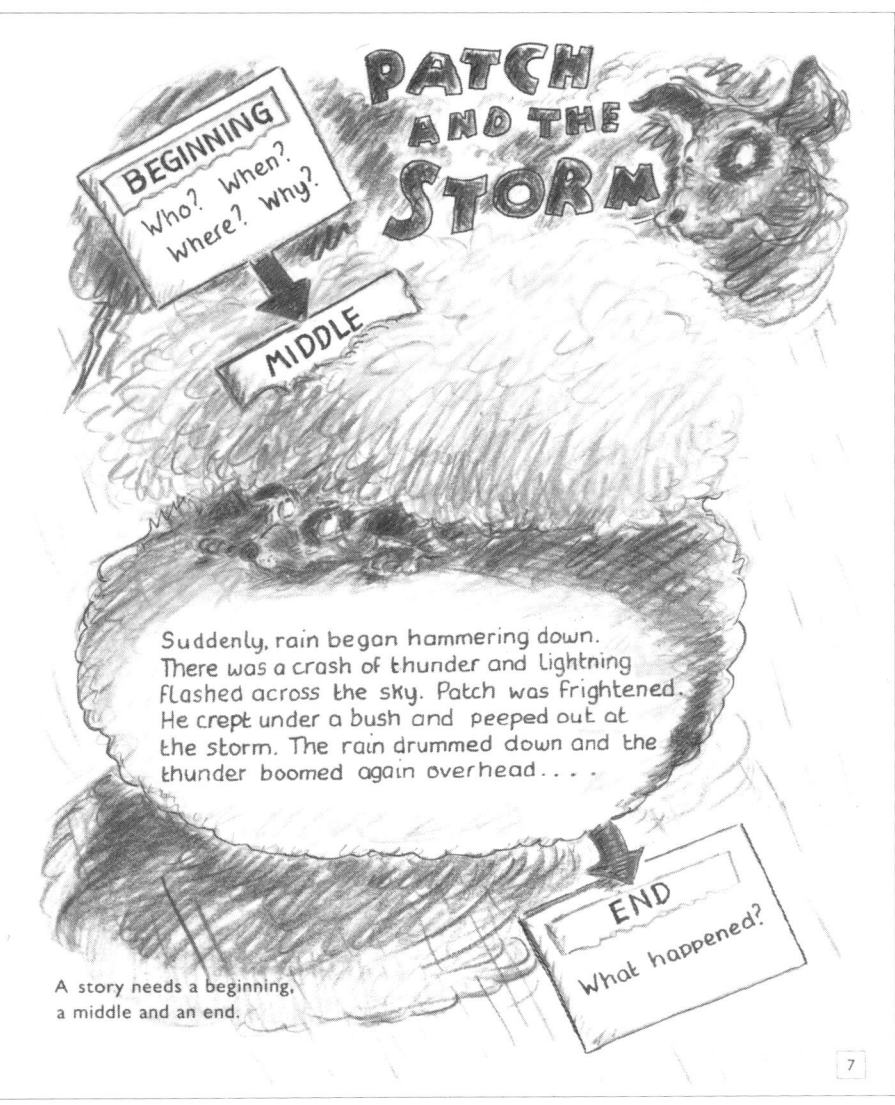

[Illustration from page 7 of Book 3: "PATCH AND THE STORM" with labels showing BEGINNING (Who? When? Where? Why?), MIDDLE, and END (What happened?). Middle caption reads: "Suddenly, rain began hammering down. There was a crash of thunder and lightning flashed across the sky. Patch was frightened. He crept under a bush and peeped out at the storm. The rain drummed down and the thunder boomed again overhead...." Below: "A story needs a beginning, a middle and an end."]

This page is intended as a focus for the development of children's **writing skills** and appreciation of **story structure**. It should be tackled in two parts on different occasions.

Session 1: Discussion/Planning

The picture and caption on page 7 of Book 3 represent the middle of a story:

- Discuss what is happening in the picture – relate to children's own experience of storms, and of being alone and frightened.
- Discuss – what should the beginning tell us, so that we will understand what is going on? (See questions on top left of picture.)
- Elicit a variety of possible beginnings.
- Each pupil now draws the beginning s/he chooses.

> Science links: thunderstorms; conduction of electricity; speed of sound and light.

Discussion/Writing: a good beginning

Discuss what makes a successful beginning in terms of writing, e.g.:
How long should the beginning be compared to the rest of the story? (NB Avoid the unnecessary detail with which many children get bogged down when starting stories – encourage pupils to 'jump straight in')
What questions should a beginning answer? (See note alongside illustration.) Look at the beginnings of some favourite books from the library. Each pupil to write a beginning for the Patch story, using own drawing as a focus. When the **beginning** is complete, s/he can write more middle, adding to/improving the picture's caption.

These pieces of writing may be retained for later use with pages 12–13.

Session 2: Discussion/Planning/Writing

The ending of a story should provide a clear resolution. Using examples of pupils' beginnings + middles, discuss:
What would be a happy ending? What would be a sad ending? What points need to be made clear/tied up?
Each pupil draws an illustration of the ending s/he wishes for own story so far. Pupils should then write their endings, focusing on their pictures.

Again writing may be retained for use with drafting/editing exercise.

Picture books
(See list for Book 2, page 3.)
Stormy Weather, Amanda Harvey (Pan/Macmillan)

Out in the cold *(page 8)*

Spoken language: relating a connected narrative

Children to work in pairs: A and B.

Picture 1 – 11:
A can see the picture story, B cannot. A to relate the story exactly to B, giving all necessary detail so that B can envisage the pictures. B to ask for more information where necessary.

> Science link: describing activities by sequencing major features

Pictures 12 – 23:
B to relate narrative, A to listen and question if necessary. (Raymond Briggs's *The Snowman* is also suitable for this activity.)

Language work: verbs and tenses

(Definition in Glossary, page 32 of Book 3)
When children attempted the above exercise, did they speak in the past or present tense (probably the present)? Help children identify that tense is a feature of verbs.
In a group, invent narrative for several frames in past/present/future tenses. Once pupils seem confident, try the following game.

Tense swapping game
Pupils each have copy of 'Out in the Cold' or other picture strip (e.g. from comic book). Going round the group, they take turns to tell the story of one frame in the strip. Before each pupil's turn, the teacher calls 'past tense' or 'present tense', and pupil must adjust verbs as necessary. This can be converted into a team game (members of opposing teams taking alternate turns, and scoring a point for the team if tense is correct).

Spoken language

Another activity which can be carried out using a picture story (e.g. pages from *The Snowman*):

Giving/Following instructions: cooperative group work

Children work in groups: some are actors and should not be able to see the pictures. One is the director, and should be looking at the pictures. The director must give the actors detailed instructions so that they can mimic the actions of the characters in the pictures exactly. They may ask for further information if they require it.
One is the judge, also with access to the pictures, who decides whether the acting is accurate enough.

(page 9)

Writing within a clearly defined framework

Pupils write an account of the little girl's activities in the picture story (or an extract from *The Snowman*, or another cartoon strip).

> Science links: effects of cold; insulation; drying; warming.

- Each pupils decides whether to write as the protagonist (I) or about the protagonist (s/he). Those choosing the latter should invent a name for their character.
- Each pupil decides whether to write in the past or present tense.
- Lists of useful vocabulary/ spelling words can be compiled on the board. These could be listed under the headings NOUNS, VERBS and ADJECTIVES, to help reinforce definitions.

Assess accounts for clarity and detail – do pupils explain the various stages in the process clearly? Have they maintained their chosen tenses?

> Science link: describing activities by sequencing major features

Language work: pronouns

'A pronoun stands in place of a noun.'
- Demonstrate by reading a passage (e.g. from page 4 of Book 3)
  a) as it is written
  b) with the character's name substituted for each pronominal reference.
  (e.g. The North Wind puffed up the North Wind's cheeks and began to blow. The North Wind blew the hats off people's heads but The North Wind didn't blow the cloak . . . etc. to 'keep himself warm in the cold north wind.') Pupils can identify which words in the text are pronouns.
- Demonstrate the difference between 'the I pronouns' and the 'S/he pronouns' by reading pieces of children's writing written in the first and third persons. Can children list some 'I' pronouns? some 'he/she/it' pronouns?
- Discuss the problem of slipping from 'I' to 's/he' or vice versa, which often happens in children's writing. Pupils can attempt to convert (orally) their own pieces of writing entirely from the person in which they have chosen to write into the alternative person.

Books

Read aloud story:
'Pooh Builds a House At Pooh Corner' from *The House At Pooh Corner*, A A Milne (Methuen)
(See also notes on books about snowy weather in Big Book, pages 7, 8, 10 and Book 2, pages 13 and 14.)
Picture story book:
The Snowman, Raymond Briggs (Hamish Hamilton)

Snow and snowmen (page 10)

Reading/Poetry

Read the poems with the children, and discuss as appropriate, including:

'If Only I Could Take Home A Snowflake'
Where do you think the speaker in this poem is? Where do you think 'home' is? Why should he want to show his friends a snowflake – where are they? Why do you think he compares snowflakes to insects?

'Icicle Joe'
Discuss snowmen, relating to children's own experience.
What happened to Icicle Joe, and why?

> Science link: change related to variation in temperature

Giving/Following instructions

Split pupils into groups A and B. Show group A how to make a six-pointed snowflake (instructions on page 109 of these Notes).

> Technology link

When they have made their own snowflakes, each member of group A passes on the instructions to a member of group B.
See also 'Making a snowstorm' (Book 2, pages 14-15) which could be adapted to use in the same way for group B to give instructions.

> Science link: crystals

Writing a poem: non-chronological writing

Apart from insects, to what else could you compare snowflakes? To what could you compare rain? sun? thunder? etc.
Use the best comparisons as the starting point for a class poem about one type of weather. If wished, pupils could then try their own comparison poems about another sort of weather.

SNOW AND SNOWMEN

If Only I Could Take Home A Snowflake

Snowflakes
like tiny
insects
drifting
down.

Without a hum
they come,
Without a hum
they go.

Snowflakes
like tiny
insects
drifting
down.

If only
I could take
one
home with me
to show
my friends
in the sun,
just for fun, –
just for fun.

John Agard

Icicle Joe

I made a snowman:
Icicle Joe.
The moon shone round him
high and low . . .
the moon shone round him
sides and back –
it gave him a shadow,
purple black.

I made a snowman
white and plump;
a nose he had
like a sugar lump.
The sun shone round him . . .
One bright day
he slumped a little
and he went away.

Vanishing softly
bit by bit
like a lollipop does
when you suck at it,
only a puddle
stayed to show
where I had built him –
Icicle Joe.

Jean Kenward

Spelling: word groups

Snow: snowman, snowflake, verb forms – snowing, snowed.
Blow: contrast verb forms – blowing, blew.
Blow is the regular one: see also grow, throw, know.

Books

Picture books:
The Snow Woman, David McKee (Beaver)
Harriet and Walt, Nancy Carson (Picture Puffin)
Happy Winter, Karen Gundersheimer (World's Work/Windmill Press)

Read aloud story (or choose an appropriate extract):
Mammy, Sugar Falling Down, Trish Cooke (Beaver)

A weather diary *(page 11)*

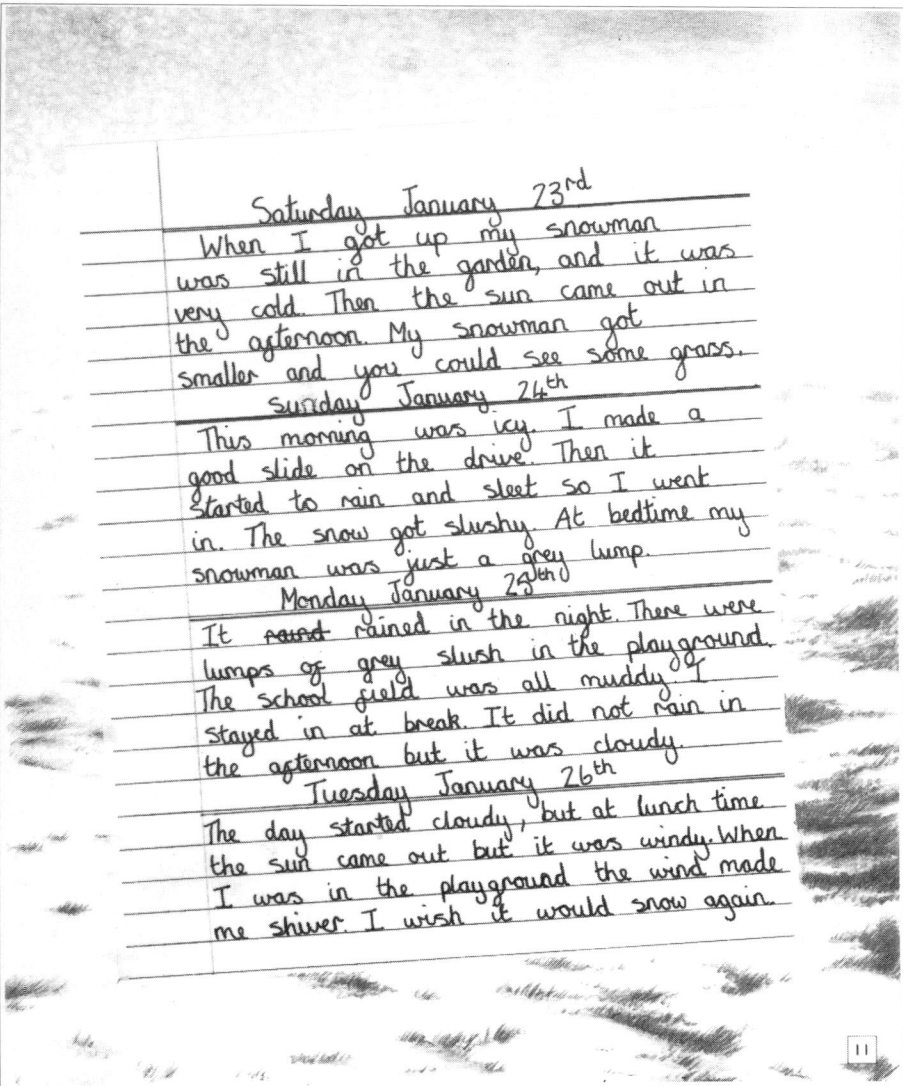

> Saturday January 23rd
> When I got up my snowman was still in the garden, and it was very cold. Then the sun came out in the afternoon. My snowman got smaller and you could see some grass.
>
> Sunday January 24th
> This morning was icy. I made a good slide on the drive. Then it started to rain and sleet so I went in. The snow got slushy. At bedtime my snowman was just a grey lump.
>
> Monday January 25th
> It rained in the night. There were lumps of grey slush in the playground. The school field was all muddy. I stayed in at break. It did not rain in the afternoon but it was cloudy.
>
> Tuesday January 26th
> The day started cloudy, but at lunch time the sun came out but it was windy. When I was in the playground the wind made me shiver. I wish it would snow again.

Report writing: keeping a diary of the week's weather

The first page of Gemma's diary is provided as a model for pupils' own weather diaries. Before embarking on writing diaries, teacher and pupils may use it as a focus for discussion/planning:

- Which is the best day to start?
- When is the best time to write your daily entry?
- What sort of things should be recorded? (Gemma has (a) described the weather (b) mentioned its effects on her own environment/behaviour.)
- How should it be set out?

> Science links: recording and interpreting observations; effects of weathering on landscape.

Handwriting

As the individual pieces of writing for the weather diary are quite short, they are ideal pieces for handwriting practice. In this case, pupils could make notes (see Glossary, page 32 of Book 3) for each entry beforehand and check on the spelling of any tricky words, so they can concentrate more fully on handwriting when writing the diary entry.

Language: tenses
Revise meaning of 'tense'. Pupils can attempt (orally) to change Gemma's diary into the present tense.

Picture book
Very simple, but enormous fun, and children might like to try writing something similar: *Mr Wolf's Week*, Colin Hawkins (Picture Lions)

3e — Language: singular and plural
(See Glossary, page 32 of Book 3.)
Worksheet 3e
Pupils should complete these individually or in pairs.

Language: singular and plural
Changing from singular to plural can effect many words – not just nouns and pronouns. Gemma is just one person – singular. Pretend two or more people had cooperated on the diary – plural. Read the diary in the plural ('When we got up...', etc.) asking pupils to help.
Put other pieces of singular writing (e.g. poem 'Icicle Joe' from page 10) on the board. Let children suggest how to change word-endings etc. to convert to the plural. And vice versa, e.g. poem 'Winter Days' on back cover (this one is quite tricky). Pupils can help collect (and list on posters) singular and plural 'I pronouns' and 'he/she pronouns':
I, me, my, myself – we, our, ours, ourselves
he, him, his, himself – they, them, their, themselves.

Drafting and editing (page 12)

This picture story is intended as a focus for discussion of the process of drafting and editing and the introduction of vocabulary. Before beginning work on this section, it will be helpful if the pupils are familiar with these metalinguistic terms:

punctuation
pronoun
tense

Other metalinguistic terms which have been covered (**noun**, **verb**, **adjective**, **singular** and **plural**) may also be useful.

Overview

Pupils should read the whole comic strip through with their teacher before discussing it.

Frames 1 and 2

Drafting and editing gives the opportunity to improve:
- correctness
- composition.

Frame 3

Discussion should elicit that Tim's work is difficult to read because of errors, e.g.:
- Missing punctuation causes difficulties with phrasing.
- Incorrect spelling disrupts fluency.
- Use of 'he' to refer to both Patch and the rabbit leads to ambiguity – so does Tim's slip into the first person in the sixth line.
- Inconsistent tenses disrupt the sense.

It could also be more explicit – e.g. 'round and round' what?

Perhaps Tim could use more adjectives and description to improve the atmosphere of his story.

Frames 4 and 5

When children read their own work they often read what they think they wrote rather than what is on the page. To avoid this Tim has left his work for a day or two (which 'distances' him from it). He is now reading it aloud (which slows him down and makes him pay more attention to the text) and a friend is following his reading and helping him to spot errors. Note the slip of paper with spelling corrections. Tim has identified words which he thinks are incorrectly spelled and requested correct spellings from his teacher.

Discuss the terms 'draft' and 'edit' to ensure children understand them. As well as editing a complete draft, children will find themselves editing work as they go along (as Tim did when he added 'a lovely' and 'day', and changed 'grey' to 'black' in his first draft).

(page 13)

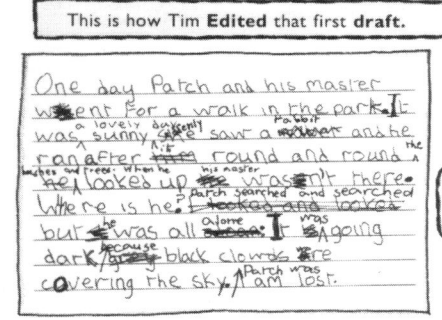

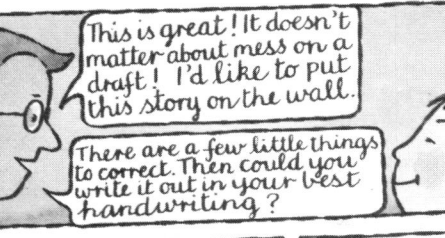

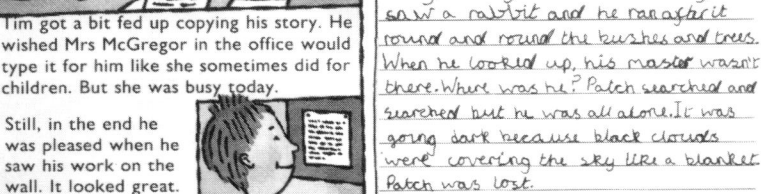

Frames 6 and 7
Many children feel that tidiness is the most important feature of written work, and are reluctant to edit because it looks scruffy. Frames 6 and 7 provide discussion material on this problem. Children can identify the changes Tim has made, and why he has made them (referring to original draft at the top of the page).
Can you spot any he has missed?

Frames 8, 9, and 10
Tim has continued to improve on his composition even at this stage. Can pupils see his final additions?

Making a fair copy of a story is often seen as a punishment, but it is an essential part of drafting and editing. As often as possible, children should be relieved of the burden of making a final copy by hand. However, fair copying is sometimes necessary and then it can be seen as an opportunity to create a beautiful piece of work, using the presentation skills children have been refining over recent months.

A comparison between Tim's original composition and this final draft shows how drafting and editing can improve a piece of writing. Comparison between the scruffy second draft and the final copy shows how attention to presentation in the final stages is worthwhile.

Drafting and editing own work

When pupils fully understand the process and purpose of drafting and editing, they can try applying their knowledge to some of their own writing. Their own short pieces on 'Patch and the Storm' may be appropriate. It is strongly recommended that children should be expected to produce work edited to this standard only occasionally.

3f Worksheet 3f: wordsearch
This worksheet includes two wordsearches, one of frequently used 'weather words', and one of words which are commonly misspelled by pupils approaching Level 3. Words can be found horizontally, vertically or diagonally and pupils should ring them as they find them.
Pupils can then be given blank wordsearch frames to make their own wordsearches (perhaps using words which they have spelled wrongly over recent weeks) for their friends to solve.

The Rat King *(page 14)*

This play provides material for group reading.
There are parts for 9 readers, but the smaller ones could if wished be doubled: e.g. Sun/Wind/Grey Rat; Cloud/Great Wall.

> Science links: the sun; effects of weathering on the landscape; air-wind; forces.

Readability levels:

Narrator	Level 2
Princess	Level 2
Rat King	Level 2+
Grand Vizier	Level 2+
Sun	Level 2
Cloud	Level 2
Wind	Level 2
Great Wall	Level 2+
Grey Rat	Level 2

Recall of the story

After first reading:
- *In which country did the Rat King live? Whereabouts did he live?*
- *To whom did the Rat King first try to marry his daughter, and why?*
- *What was the Sun's reason for refusing?*
- *Who was next, and why did he refuse?* (and so on.)

THE RAT KING

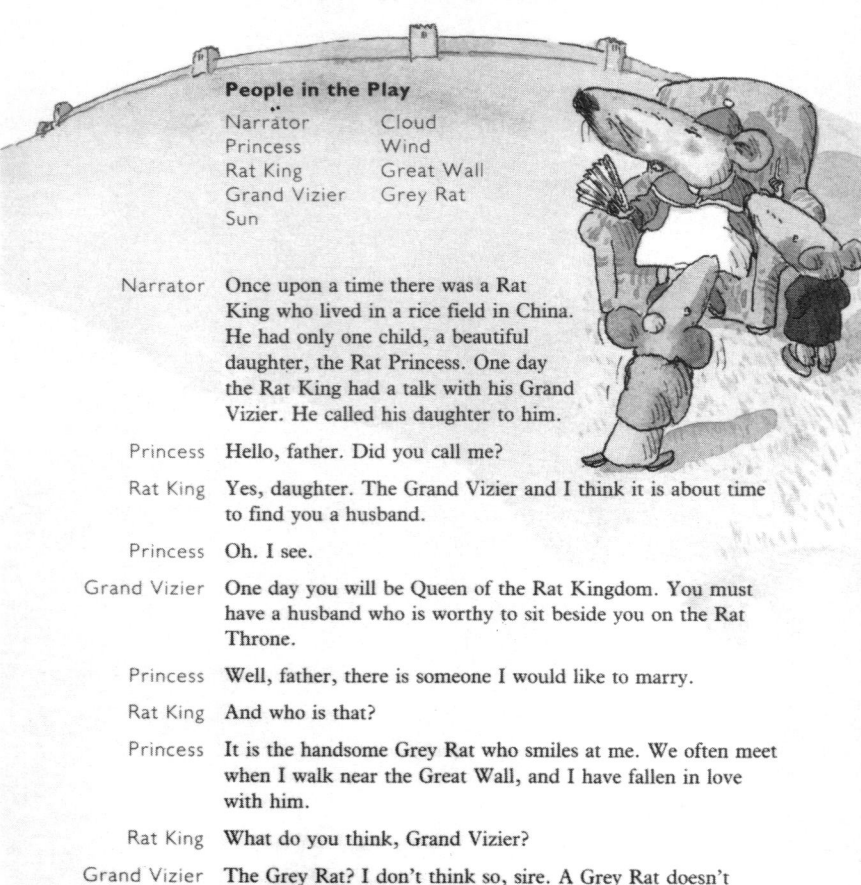

People in the Play
Narrator, Cloud
Princess, Wind
Rat King, Great Wall
Grand Vizier, Grey Rat
Sun

Narrator Once upon a time there was a Rat King who lived in a rice field in China. He had only one child, a beautiful daughter, the Rat Princess. One day the Rat King had a talk with his Grand Vizier. He called his daughter to him.

Princess Hello, father. Did you call me?

Rat King Yes, daughter. The Grand Vizier and I think it is about time to find you a husband.

Princess Oh. I see.

Grand Vizier One day you will be Queen of the Rat Kingdom. You must have a husband who is worthy to sit beside you on the Rat Throne.

Princess Well, father, there is someone I would like to marry.

Rat King And who is that?

Princess It is the handsome Grey Rat who smiles at me. We often meet when I walk near the Great Wall, and I have fallen in love with him.

Rat King What do you think, Grand Vizier?

Grand Vizier The Grey Rat? I don't think so, sire. A Grey Rat doesn't sound important enough for a king's daughter.

14

Inference from the text/Expression in reading

- *What sort of character is the Rat King?* (Children's responses to such a question are usually far from concise. However, the teacher can attempt to summarise them with suitable adjectives, which could be added to the adjective bank (see notes with page 4), e.g.: proud, pompous, fussy, swanky, grand, royal, vain, easily-influenced, bossy, impatient, bored, irritable.)
  What sort of character is the Grand Vizier? (flattering, snobbish, weak, apologetic, worried, anxious)
  What sort of character is the Princess? (meek, obedient, dutiful, fed up, discontented, grudging, worried, happy, satisfied, thrilled)
- *What sort of voices should they have?*
- *What do you think the Sun, the Cloud, the Wind and the Great Wall think of the Rat King? Why? (Can you find evidence in what they say?)*
- *What sort of voices should they have?*
- *Who do you think is the most powerful character in the play? Why?*

> Science link: voice production (sound/vibration)

(page 15)

Rat King	You're right. My daughter must marry someone powerful and important. We shall find the most powerful person in the world, and he shall be your husband.
Princess	But father . . .
Rat King	No buts, girl. Now, Grand Vizier, who or what is more powerful than anything else in the world?
Grand Vizier	Well, Your Majesty, I think it is the Sun. He gives light and heat to all the world, and everybody looks up to him.
Rat King	That is true. Well done, Grand Vizier. The Rat Princess shall marry the Sun.
Princess	But I don't want to marry the Sun. I want to marry the handsome Grey Rat who smiles at me.
Rat King	Hush, girl. I have made up my mind. Make everything ready for a journey to the home of the Sun.
Narrator	So the Rat King, the Rat Princess and the Grand Vizier went up to the home of the Sun. The Sun welcomed them.
Sun	Welcome, Rat King. It is good to see you. What brings you so far from your home in the rice field?
Rat King	I have decided that it is time for my daughter to marry, Lord Sun. I asked my Grand Vizier who was the most powerful person in the world, and he said it was you. So I have come to offer you my daughter's hand in marriage.

Discussion: language

- Different words for the same thing:
  How many ways does the Rat King tell his daughter to be quiet? (Hush, be quiet, silence, hold your tongue)
  Can you think of any others? Can you think of a variety of ways of telling someone to hurry up/stop what they're doing?
- *What do the following expressions mean?*
  'offer someone's hand in marriage', 'to be worthy of something', 'to be honoured by something', 'Grand vizier'
- Titles of respect. *What special names does the Grand Vizier use to address the Rat King to show her respect?* (Your Majesty, Sire)
  How does the Rat King address the Sun, Cloud, Wind, Wall? (Lord)
  What other titles do you know which people use to show respect when they speak (Sir, Miss, Mr…, Mrs…, Your Highness, etc.) *and to whom would they use them?*

Story structure

- *How would you split this story into beginning/middle/end?*
- *What is there about this story which makes it like a fairy tale?* (e.g. 'Once upon a time'/ 'happily ever after'/talking animals)
- *Did you work out what was going to happen before you read to the end? If so, when did you work it out, and what clues told you?*
- *What other fairy stories build up in this way, so that you can almost guess what will happen?* (e.g. Three Little Pigs, Goldilocks)

Language: complete sentences

(See Glossary: **phrases** and **sentences**, page 33 of Book 3.) When writing, pupils should generally use complete sentences. However, when people are speaking they often use phrases rather than sentences.

In this play, there are both sentences and phrases. Help children to spot the obvious phrases (i.e. those which do not contain a verb, such as 'The Grey Rat?'/'No buts, girl'/'Oh good'/'Oh no!' and various short greetings).

(page 16)

Sun	That is very kind of you, Rat King. But I am afraid you are mistaken. I am not the most powerful person in the world. There is someone who is more powerful than I.
Grand Vizier	Really? Who is that?
Sun	It is the Cloud. If the Cloud passes in front of my face, he stops my light and heat from reaching the world. There is nothing I can do to stop him. So the Cloud must be more powerful than I.
Rat King	Oh, I see. Then you were wrong, Grand Vizier.
Grand Vizier	I'm sorry, your majesty. I had not thought of that. Of course the Cloud must be more powerful than the Sun.
Princess	But I don't want to marry the Cloud. I want to marry the handsome Grey Rat who smiles at me.
Rat King	Be quiet, girl! The Cloud shall be your husband.
Narrator	So the Rat King, the Rat Princess and the Grand Vizier went to find the home of the Cloud. When they got there, the Cloud welcomed them.
Cloud	Good afternoon, Rat King. How lovely to see you. But why are you so far from your home in the rice field?
Rat King	We are seeking a husband for my daughter, Lord Cloud. I think she should marry the most powerful person in the world.
Grand Vizier	We have been to see the Sun, my lord. He says that you are more powerful than he, because you can block off his light and heat from the world.
Rat King	So I am here to offer you my daughter's hand in marriage.
Cloud	Well, that is very kind of you. She is indeed a most beautiful princess. But I am afraid that there is someone more powerful than I.

16

3g

Worksheet 3g: how to answer in sentences
Responding to comprehension questions gives pupils an opportunity to look at how sentences are formed. Section A of the worksheet provides three questions about 'The Rat King'. For the first question the answer is provided as a phrase (in the speech bubble) and as a sentence (handwritten on the line). The latter provides a model for completing the remaining sentence answers in Section A.

Pupils who have only recently reached Level 2 will need much teacher-support to grasp the point of this.

Once pupils seem secure, Section B gives questions about 'The Rat King' which pupils should answer in complete sentences.

3h

Worksheet 3h: sentence punctuation
This worksheet consists of two short passages for punctuation – one fiction and one non-fiction – which can be cut up for use on separate occasions. Pupils could either 'correct' the worksheet, or copy out each passage adding punctuation. Alternatively, the passages could be transferred to a file on Pendown or other word-processing package.

Science link

(page 17)

Grand Vizier	Oh no! Who is it?
Cloud	It is the Wind. He can blow me anywhere he likes. I have no power against the Wind.
Grand Vizier	Oh, that is true. I had not thought of that. Of course the Wind must be more powerful than the Cloud.
Rat King	You don't seem to have thought very much at all. I'm beginning to wish I had not asked your advice. Come, we'd better visit the Wind and offer the princess to him.
Princess	But I don't want to marry the Wind. I want to marry the handsome Grey Rat who smiles at me.
Rat King	Silence, girl! The Wind shall be your husband. Let us make ready to visit him.
Narrator	The Rat King, the Rat Princess, and the Grand Vizier went to the home of the Wind, and explained again how they were looking for a husband for the Rat Princess.
Wind	I am very pleased to see you, Rat King. And I am very pleased that you have chosen me. But I have to tell you that there is someone more powerful than I.
Grand Vizier	Oh no!
Rat King	There can't be!
Wind	I am afraid there is. It is the Great Wall of China. He is tall and strong. No matter how hard I blow, I cannot blow down the Great Wall. I cannot even move him. The Great Wall of China is far stronger than I.
Rat King	What do you say to this, Grand Vizier!
Grand Vizier	Oh, your majesty, I had not thought of it. Of course the Great Wall must be more powerful than the Wind. I was wrong again.

17

Group work: presentation
Once pupils are familiar with the play, groups could attempt presentations of it. There are various possibilities.

(Technology link)

Taped reading
A taped presentation could involve the production of a musical introduction/accompaniment and sound effects.

Puppet play
The characters could be made from sock puppets or stick puppets and the Sun, Wind, Cloud, Great Wall could be cut-outs mounted on sticks. The puppet theatre could be simply covered tables, or a more elaborate arrangement. Pupils could work in pairs to make puppets; then one could operate the puppets as the other reads the lines.

Staged play
A staged presentation, perhaps for another class, could also involve the design and production of appropriate masks/costumes for the characters.

Information Technology
Any production of the play provides an opportunity for the design of a programme, using Pendown or other desk-top publishing package.

Science link: storage and retrieval on computer.

Dramatisation of stories
The folktale given on pages 93 – 94, or 'The Twelve Months' (109 – 111) would both be suitable for dramatisation by groups of pupils.

(page 18)

Rat King	Then my daughter must marry the Great Wall.
Princess	But I don't want to marry the Great Wall. I want to marry the handsome Grey Rat who smiles at me!
Rat King	Hold your tongue, girl! I'm getting fed up of all this. We shall go to the Great Wall and offer him your hand in marriage.
Narrator	So the Rat King, the Rat Princess and the Grand Vizier went to visit the Great Wall of China, and yet again the Rat King offered his daughter's hand in marriage.
Great Wall	It is very kind of you to visit me, Rat King. I am very pleased to see you. And I am honoured that you have offered your daughter to be my bride. But why have you chosen me?
Rat King	You explain, Grand Vizier. I'm too tired.
Grand Vizier	Well, Lord Wall. The Rat King wishes his daughter to marry someone who is more powerful than anyone else on earth. First we went to the Sun, but he said the Cloud was more powerful than he. Then we went to the Cloud, but he said the Wind was more powerful than he. Then we went to the Wind, but he said you were more powerful than he. I hope there is no one more powerful than you.
Rat King	So do I.
Great Wall	Well, I am very powerful indeed. No wind or weather can shake me. I have stood here for hundreds of years.
Rat King	Good, good.
Great Wall	But . . .
Rat King	Oh no!

Folk literature
The theme of 'The Rat King' is echoed in this folktale from Thailand.

The dog who wanted to be the sun
There was once a little dog called Sammy, who thought he could do everything better than everyone else. So one day he looked up at the sun and shouted: 'I want to swap places with you! I'd be good at shining. Why not let me be the sun, and I'll shine all day, and you can come down here and be a little dog?' The sun smiled to himself at Sammy's self-importance, 'All right,' he said, 'I'll grant your wish. Come on!'

So Sammy swapped places with the sun, and went up in the sky to shine on the earth. Unfortunately, he wasn't as good as he thought he'd be. He shone and shone and shone, until everyone on earth was fainting with heat, all the plants were withering, and the rivers and streams were drying up.

People got angry and shouted at the real sun to complain. 'Oh dear,' said the sun. 'But I know how to stop him.' And the sun called to the big black cloud who lived in the north of the sky.

The big black cloud rolled in front of Sammy-the-Sun, and everyone on earth heaved a sigh of relief. But Sammy was fed up. He complained to the sun. 'I don't want to be you if I can't shine,' he said. 'I'd rather be the big black cloud. I could be bigger and blacker than any cloud there has ever been.'

'All right,' said the sun, and he went back to his own place, and let Sammy swap places with the big black cloud. Sammy rolled about the heavens thoroughly enjoying himself. He swelled up and covered the whole sky, and not a single ray of sunlight could pass through. The whole world was plunged into darkness and cold so that the plants couldn't grow and all the people and animals were very frightened.

Everyone began to shout at the sun again, so he called to the strong wind who lived in the east of the sky, and the wind blew Sammy-the-Cloud until he no longer covered the sun.

> Science links: heat and cold; light; air → wind.

(page 19)

Great Wall	There is one creature who can damage me. He has lived for years in the ground beneath me, and has nibbled and gnawed at my bricks so that some of them have begun to crumble. I fear that, in the whole world, he is the only creature more powerful than I.
Princess	Who is he? Who is he?
Great Wall	He is the Grey Rat.
Grand Vizier	Oh dear, dear me. I hadn't thought of that. Of course the Grey Rat must be more powerful than the Wall.
Princess	Yes, of course he must!
Narrator	At that moment, from a hole beneath the Great Wall there appeared a handsome Grey Rat. He smiled at the princess and she smiled shyly back.
Grey Rat	Good day, Your Majesty! Did I hear someone speaking my name?
Great Wall	His Majesty the Rat King is looking for a powerful husband for the Rat Princess. I have just told him how powerful you are.
Grand Vizier	There isn't anyone more powerful than you, is there?
Grey Rat	Not that I can think of.
Rat King	In that case, Lord Grey Rat, I should like to offer you my daughter's hand in marriage.
Grey Rat	I am honoured, your majesty.
Princess	Oh thank you, father.
Narrator	So the Grey Rat and the Rat Princess were married, and the Sun, the Cloud, the Wind and the Great Wall all came to the wedding to wish them luck.
Everyone	Good luck, Grey Rat and your bride.
Princess	And now my handsome Grey Rat and I can live happily ever after!

Discussion

How are 'The Rat King' and 'The dog who wanted to be the sun' alike? How are they different?
Which of the characters in the play/the story could talk in real life?
Which do you think it is silliest to have talking in a story? Why?
What other folktales do you know in which (a) animals, (b) non-living things can talk?

Science link: characteristics of living things

Sammy was angry again. 'Let me swap places with the wind,' he asked the sun. 'I'd be really good at blowing.' So the sun let Sammy swap places with the wind and Sammy-the-Wind blew with all his might. He blew the leaves off the trees, he blew the plants out of the ground, he blew the buildings off their foundations. The terrified people yelled again to the sun to stop him, but the sun couldn't hear for the noise of Sammy blowing.

Then one day, Sammy found something that he couldn't blow down. It was an anthill which the white ants had built so skilfully that it was impossible to blow over. 'That's good,' thought Sammy to himself, 'but I bet I could do it better.' So now Sammy shouted at the sun: 'I want to be the anthill.' 'All right,' said the sun. 'You can be the anthill.'

So Sammy became Sammy-the-Anthill and felt very strong, until one day a water buffalo came running past and knocked the anthill over with his flailing hooves. 'I want to be a water-buffalo!' screamed Sammy furiously. 'All right,' sighed the sun, wondering how much longer this was going to go on.

The next day, a farmer's boy came along and threw a rope round the water-buffalo's neck. 'I want to be a piece of rope!' yelled Sammy, and the sun immediately changed him into one.

But no sooner had Sammy-the-Rope got used to his new form and started feeling strong and powerful, than a little dog came running out from the farm and began playing about, throwing the rope into the air and tearing at it with his teeth. 'I want to be a little dog!' yelled Sammy. 'I'd be really good at being a little dog!' 'Thank goodness!' said the sun. He turned Sammy back into a little dog again. 'I think that's what you're best at.' he said. 'So that's how you'll stay!'

Science link: forces

Technology link: wind resistance

Science link: cycles (see page 24)

Reading for information *(page 20)*

This picture story provides a stimulus for discussion of the processes involved in reading for information and introduces the vocabulary required to talk about it. IT IS NOT AN ALTERNATIVE TO REAL INFORMATION SEARCH AND READING.

Once discussion is over, pupils must engage in the process themselves. It is therefore important that enough suitable information books are available for the group's use (we recommend a minimum of 2 books per pupil). On the whole, the reading level of information books should be a little lower than that with which pupils cope in narrative material.

Overview
Pupils should read the whole picture story through with the teacher before discussing individual frames.

Reading/Discussion
More detailed reading and discussion would best be done in two parts:
- frames 1 – 6 (followed by an opportunity for pupils to browse themselves)
- frames 7 – 15 (followed by an opportunity for pupils to find answers to their own questions).

Frame 1
Children working towards Level 3 should be aware of the difference between 'story books' and 'fact books' (use Worksheet 2e, if required).
Ensure pupils understand the terms 'fiction' and 'non-fiction'. (Definitions in glossary: opportunity for discussion apropos wall poster shown in this frame.)

Frames 2 – 5
There is a great deal of new vocabulary here. Definitions of **captions**, **headings**, **sub-headings**, and **keywords** are given in the Glossary (page 32 of Book 3). The illustrations in these frames should help pupils learn these new words. However, discussion and opportunities to find examples in real non-fiction books in the classroom are essential to understanding.
- Treasure Hunt in classroom project books:
  *Can you find a book with a Contents Page?
  a picture with a caption?
  a chapter heading
  (and the reference to it in the Contents)?
  a sub-heading?*
- Keywords: *What are some keywords about weather?*

(page 21)

Frame 6
This frame shows children becoming involved in browsing, and thus acquiring some of the background knowledge they require to think about the subject for themselves.

At this point, pupils should have the opportunity to browse in the class project collection.

Frame 7: formulating questions
Questions have already been covered from other angles in 'Questions of Weather' (page 6 of Book 3) and Worksheet 3c. See also '**statements**' and '**questions**' in Glossary on page 33 of Book 3.

Formulating good questions for information-finding purposes is not easy. To some extent, you need to know the answers before you can formulate the questions.

Science links: hypothesising; formulating questions.

One way round this is to ask each pupil to write down a good question about the weather to which, as a result of browsing, s/he already knows the answer. Questions can then be vetted and doled out to other pupils, so that they can try to track the answers down.

Frames 8 and 9
Vocabulary: **title**, **contents page** (these are not included in the Glossary). Most good children's information books these days include a contents page. Its use is fairly straightforward and can be practised, if necessary, using the contents page of this book.

(page 22)

Frames 10, 11 and 12
Vocabulary: **index**, **keywords** (both in Glossary), **alphabetical order**.
Practice of alphabetical order is given in Worksheet 2f.
After discussion, practice in locating keywords in an index, and in using these to find the appropriate pages in a book, is given in **Worksheet 3h**.

Frame 13
Vocabulary: **skim**, **scan** (both in Glossary, page 32 of Book 3).
Pupils should have already begun to skim and scan. They were probably skimming rapidly through books during their browsing period, and using an index involves scanning for keywords.

The application of these reading modes to text can really only be developed through practice. Thus, the more questions pupils attempt to answer, the more skilled they are likely to become.

Frames 14 and 15
When the relevant section of text is identified, careful attentive reading is required, and pupils must reflect on what they read to ensure their full understanding of the words and concepts concerned. Again, this is a very different sort of 'reading' from that involved in enjoying a story. The test of pupils' success in reading for information is their subsequent ability to answer questions on the topic without reference to the book. At Level 3, such retailing of information learned is probably best done orally.

Once children have learned the elements involved in reading for information, the teacher should take every opportunity to encourage its use. When questions arise within the project, pupils should seek answers in the books available. Whenever a new topic is introduced, relevant non-fiction books should be provided, and the skills demonstrated here applied.

Clouds and rain *(page 23)*

Clouds

Wonder where they come from?
Wonder where they go?
Wonder why they're sometimes high
and sometimes hanging low?
Wonder what they're made of,
and if they weigh a lot?
Wonder if the sky feels bare
up there
   when clouds are *not*?

Aileen Fisher

Where does the rain come from?

What are clouds made of?

CLOUDS AND RAIN

There is lots of water on the earth. There is water in the sea, in rivers, in lakes, in puddles. When the sun shines, it warms the water up.

When water gets hot it evaporates into the air. You cannot see it evaporating. It is called water vapour. The water vapour rises up into the sky.

When the water vapour gets high up it starts to get cold again. It turns back into little drops of water. A lot of tiny drops of water gathered together make a cloud up in the sky. Now you know where clouds come from!

Sometimes the little drops of water touch each other. Then they join together to make bigger drops. The bigger drops are heavy.

When the drops are too heavy to float in the air, they start to fall down. It starts to rain! The rain falls to the earth. It falls into the sea, into rivers, into lakes, into puddles.

Then the sun comes out and the story starts all over again!

The 'Clouds' poem can be read as an introduction to the 'Clouds and Rain' exercise below.

Poetry/Reading/Group presentation

Later readings:
Try a reading in several voices, one for each question, spoken slowly and wonderingly, but following on from each other quite rapidly. (Ask each reader to start his/her question as the last reader is saying his/her final word.) Readers can emphasise the questioning tone in their voices.
Groups of five could each prepare a presentation for the class, for discussion of/voting on the most successful.

Reading non-fiction material

'Clouds and Rain'
In 'Reading for information' we presented a model for the process of children's information search. The final frames describe the intensive reading required once relevant material is located. In this section we provide a short piece of non-fiction material on which intensive reading methods can be practised.

Questions, explicitness, factual information

Two questions are suggested by the poem at the top of the page:
- What are clouds made of?
- Where does rain come from?

Pupils should read the passage and, in their own words, give oral answers to these questions.
They can then make up more questions inspired by the passage (e.g. Where do puddles come from? What is evaporation?) and frame clear, explicit answers.

When the passage has been read in depth, proceed to page 24 of Book 3.

> Science link: water cycle; heat and cold; change.

Picture books
About clouds:
see notes to Book 2, page 5.

Sun and Rain/Rainy nights (page 24)

Reading a diagram
What is a diagram? (See Glossary, page 32 of Book 3.) *What information in the writing on the previous page is missing from this diagram? How does the diagram show the order in which things happen?* etc.
This is a cycle-diagram. *Can you think why it's called that? What other cycles can you think of which could be represented in this way?*

Spoken explanation, factual explicitness
In pairs, pupils explain to each other exactly what is happening in the pictures (taking alternate ones). They should not look back at the passage.

> Science links: interpreting diagrams; cycles, including human life cycle.

Written factual information
Pupils next write a simple explanation of the water cycle. Again, they should use the diagrams as a stimulus and not look back at the previous page. This exercise develops a pupil's confidence to write using his/her own words, rather than copy verbatim from a non-fiction text. (This might be a suitable piece for drafting and editing to achieve maximum explicitness.)

Diagrams and writing
Teachers may find it helpful in other information finding/recording activities to ask pupils to represent what they have learned pictorially in the first instance. Their pictures then become the stimulus for written accounts.

Hymn
The hymn 'Glad That I Live Am I', in many primary school hymn books, provides a view of the water cycle from another angle.

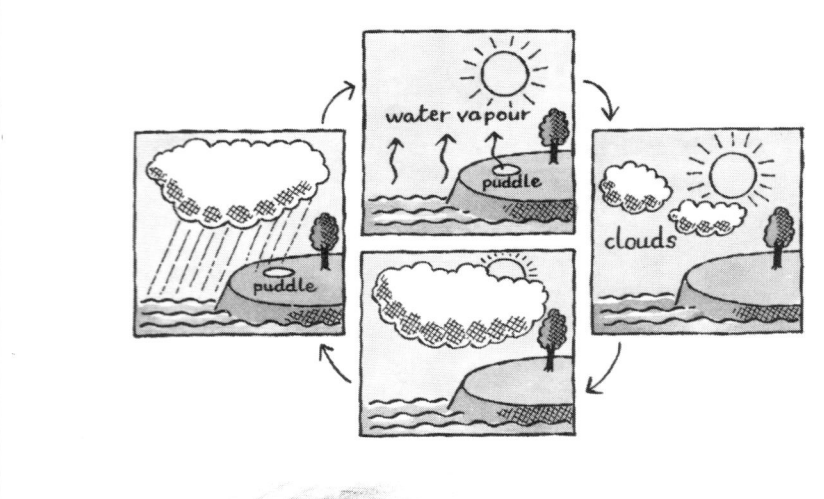

Rainy Nights

I like the town on rainy nights
  When everything is wet –
When all the town has magic lights
  And streets of shining jet!

When all the rain about the town
  Is like a looking-glass,
And all the lights are upside-down
  Below me as I pass.

In all the pools are velvet skies,
  And down the dazzling street
A fairy city gleams and lies
  In beauty at my feet.

Irene Thomspon

Poem: Discussion/Language
Rainy Nights
What is jet? What is a looking glass? What is velvet? What are the textures of these three things? Which textures do you think are best to compare with a wet road?
This poem has a strong rhyme scheme, known as A B A B. Can the pupils work out what this means? Can they find other poems in the book which rhyme/don't rhyme? Which do they prefer, and why?

> Science links: light and reflections; mirrors.

Books about rain
See notes to Big Book, pages 11, 12, 13, 14, and Book 2, pages 9, 21, 22 and 23.
Story which pupils nearing Level 3 can read for themselves:
'A Necklace of Raindrops' from *A Necklace of Raindrops and Other Stories,* Joan Aiken (Puffin)

Read aloud story:
'Piglet Is Entirely Surrounded by Water' in *Winnie the Pooh,* AA Milne (Methuen)

Splash! *(page 25)*

> **SPLASH!**
>
> I am sitting
> In the middle
> Of a rather Muddy
> Puddle,
> With my bottom
> Full of bubbles
> And my wellies
> Full of Mud.
>
> While my jacket
> And my sweater
> Go on slowly
> Getting wetter
> As I very
> Slowly settle
> To the Bottom
> Of the Mud.
>
> And I find that
> What a person
> With a puddle
> Round his middle
> Thinks of mostly
> In the muddle
> Is the Muddi-
> Ness of Mud.
>
> Dennis Lee

First reading of poem: for pleasure and discussion as appropriate. Move immediately to writing exercise below. Later readings: this poem is particularly easy for learning by heart, and very satisfying to chant. The poet's use of capital letters (technically incorrect) is interesting to discuss.

> Science links: investigation of natural material (soil); characteristics of materials (effects of water).

Descriptive writing/Story structure

The poem is provided as a stimulus for a structured piece of descriptive personal writing. It should be carried out over two sessions.

> **Story**
> Pupils nearing Level 3 could read for themselves: 'Timothy Puddle', HE Todd, in *Bad Boys,* ed. Eileen Colwell (Puffin)

Session 1
Lead discussion on to the subject of 'getting wet' – pupil's own experience (could be unpleasant, e.g. falling in a puddle, drenched in a rainstorm, or pleasant, e.g. at the swimming pool, in the sea).
Each pupil to:
- draw/paint a picture of When I Got Wet
- collect (either round the picture or on scrap paper) as many words and phrases as possible to summon up:
  – what they could feel
  – what they could hear
  – what they could smell
  – what they could taste/see/touch
  – their feelings inside
- using these notes, produce a detailed piece of writing describing what is happening in the picture (NOT the events leading up to it, or afterwards). This passage could be redrafted and improved if necessary.

> Science links: the senses; observation.

Session 2 (optional)
The passage produced above should provide the middle section of a story. Look back to 'Patch and the Storm'.
Each child to write:
- a beginning, answering the who, when, where, why questions;
- an end, explaining what happened next (e.g. getting dry).

Provide wall posters to jog memories:

> What could you FEEL?   HEAR?
>   SMELL? SEE?
>   TASTE? TOUCH?
> What were your FEELINGS INSIDE?

> BEGINNING →
> Who?
> When?   MIDDLE → END
> Where?   What happened?
> Why?

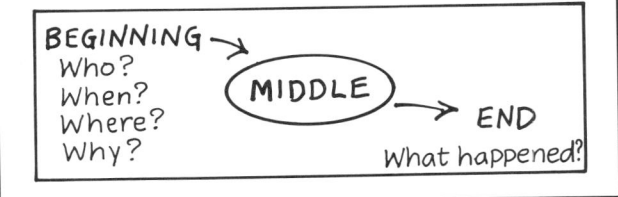

WEATHER BOOK 3

A letter from India *(page 26)*

(Readability: Level 2+)
The letter is from a boy in India to his female cousin in Britain.

Reading/Discussion
Read the letter with the group and discuss, e.g.: *This letter is obviously a reply – who wrote first? What do you think she asked and why?*
Where is India? (Atlas/any books in the library with pictures?)
Does anyone have any relations in India? Is it hotter or colder than Britain? What do you think a monsoon is?
What do you notice about the name and address of the writer? Would you say it rains all year round in Britain? How would you describe our weather? etc. (Poem on page 27 of Book 3 provides a framework for discussion of British weather month by month.)

Language: proper nouns
(See Glossary, page 33 of Book 3.) Names and addresses are obvious examples of proper nouns. After looking at the example on the envelope, each pupil should write:
- own name and address
- best friend's name and address with particular attention to layout and capital letters for proper nouns.

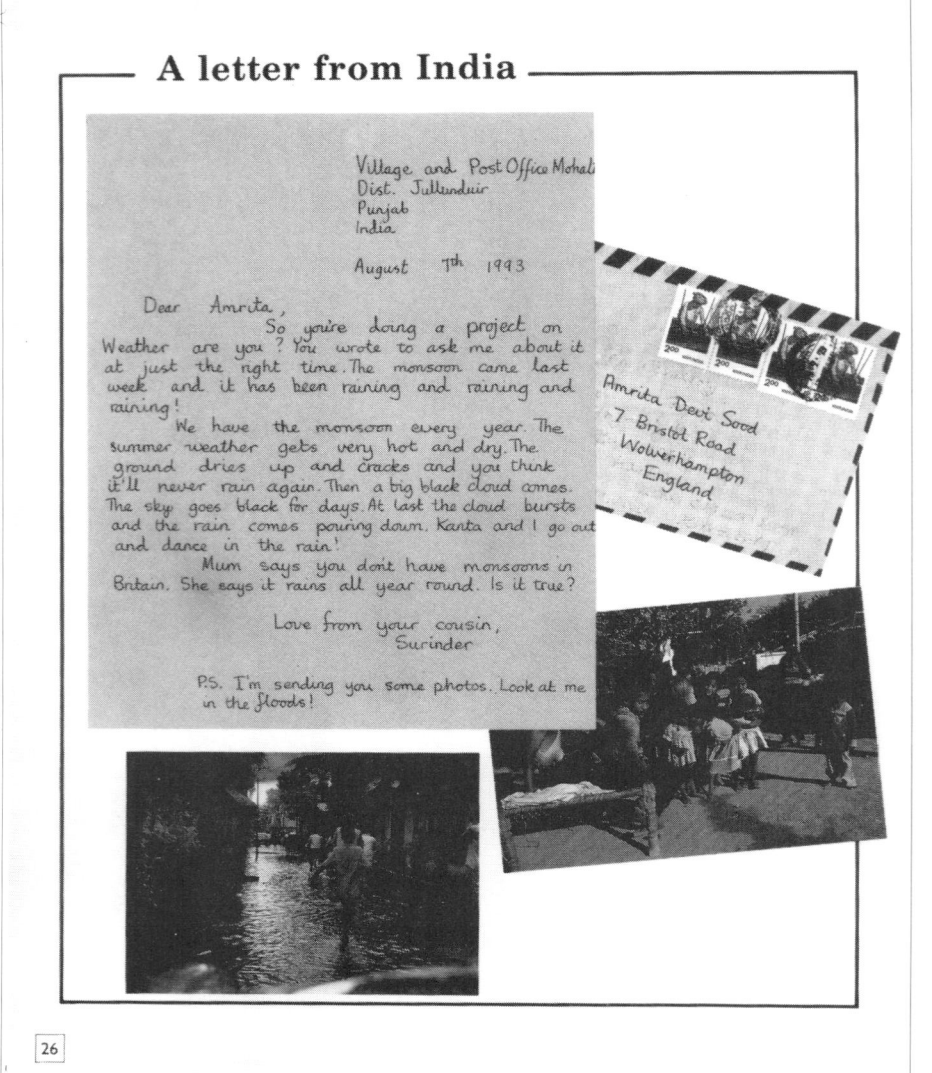

Letter writing
If pupils do not have any relatives abroad whom they can contact, as Amrita obviously has, you can establish links with schools in other countries through the Commonwealth Linking Trust, 7 Lion Yard, Tremadoc Road, London, SW4 7NF, 071 498 1101.
Genuine writing opportunities of this kind are ideal for teaching letter-writing skills. The letter from Surinder provides a model for layout, etc., which should be discussed at length before pupils are expected to produce their own letters:
- own address in top right-hand corner
- date beneath it
- Dear_____, and indentation of first line of letter
- layout of letter, 'signing off line' and signature.

Discuss suitable 'signing off lines' for particular circumstances ('Best wishes', 'Love', 'All the best', etc. in a personal letter of this kind). Surinder's envelope similarly provides a model for addressing an envelope.

Picture book
Bringing the Rain to Kapiti Plain, V Aardama (Macmillan)

Around the year (page 27)

> Winter: slippy, drippy, nippy.
>
> **Around the Year**
>
> January brings the snow,
>   Makes our feet and fingers glow;
> February brings the rain,
>   Thaws the frozen lake again;
> March brings breezes loud and shrill,
>   Stirs the dancing daffodil.
>
> April brings the primrose sweet,
>   Scatters daisies at our feet;
> May brings flocks of pretty lambs,
>   Skipping by their fleecy dams;
> June brings tulips, lilies, roses,
>   Fills the children's hands with posies.
>
> Hot July brings cooling showers,
>   Apricots and gillyflowers;
> August brings the sheaves of corn,
>   Then the harvest home is borne;
> Warm September brings the fruit,
>   Sportsmen then begin to shoot.
>
> Fresh October brings the pheasant,
>   Then to gather nuts is pleasant;
> Dull November brings the blast,
>   Then the leaves are whirling fast;
> Chill December brings the sleet,
>   Blazing fire and Christmas treat.
>
> Sara Coleridge
>
> Autumn: wheezy, sneezy, freezy.
> Spring is showery, flowery, bowery.
> Summer: hoppy, croppy, poppy.

Language

The short poem written around the outside of the illustrations uses three rhyming words to describe each season. Do pupils recognise that most of these are adjectives? (See 'Spelling/Language' notes to page 6.) Some words, however, might be other parts of speech: 'poppy' could be an adjective (about the popping of seeds? or fizzy pop?) or it could be a noun (the summer flower).

Discussion: seasons in the Southern Hemisphere

Look back to 'Summer and Winter', page 2 of Book 3. Michael Dugan is an Australian poet, and the summer and winter he refers to are the Australian ones. Do the pupils know that seasons are reversed in the Southern Hemisphere? e.g. *Which season would it be now? In which season would Christmas fall?*

(Science links: inclination of the sun; sun and earth.)

(Readability: approximately Level 3/4)
Pupils should be able to read parts of the poem after hearing the teacher's reading.

Reading with expression

Try splitting the poem up for 12 voices, each attempting to convey qualities of the month within voice tone.

Discussion

Are all children sure of the order of months/number of days in each? The illustration shows the year as a cycle: relate back to the water cycle.
Which months fit into each season?

(Science links: response of living things to seasonal changes; inclination of the sun.)

Listening/Prediction

See the story 'The Twelve Months' – page 107 of these Teacher's Notes.

(Science link: cycles)

Cooperative group work

Twelve groups to produce collage pictures of the months, emphasising weather aspects, for display in cycle format. Discuss colours/textures/shapes appropriate to each month. The relevant lines from the poem could be written on each picture.

Language: proper nouns

NB Months' names, like days of week, are proper nouns.

Books

Picture books:
The Bad Babies' Book of Months, Tony Bradman (Piccadilly Press)
Chicken Soup with Rice: A Book Of Months, Maurice Sendak (Harper & Row)

Story for pupils to read by themselves:
'Spring' in *Frog and Toad Are Friends*, Arnold Lobel (Puffin I Can Read)

What is a rainbow? *(page 28)*

(Readability: Level 3)

Reading/Listening/Recall of details

The story should first be read aloud to the pupils. Discuss as appropriate, including:
- *What did Beth first think had caused the rainbow?*
- *Who did she ask about it first?*
- *What did her grandmother say the rainbow was?*
- *Who did Beth ask next?*
- *What did he say the rainbow was?*
- *Who did she ask next/what did he say?*
- *Who was Sam?*
- *What did he say about the rainbow?*

> Science links: reflection; colour spectrum.

Discussion/Story structure

Beginning: section 1 – seeing the rainbow
Middle: development over 3 sections –
   Gran's explanation
   Vicar's explanation
   Dad's explanation
End: final section – summary and Sam's summing up.
- Can the pupils identify these elements?
- What device does the writer use to conclude each of the middle sections and the final section of the story?

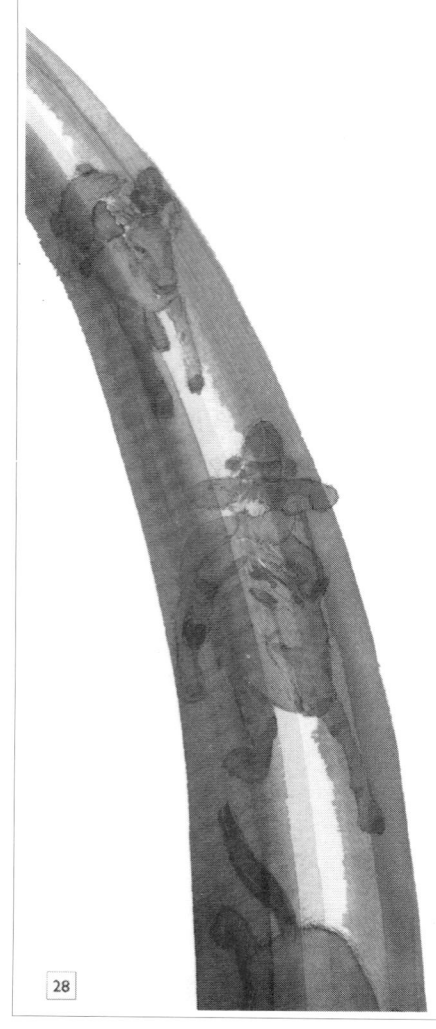

WHAT IS A RAINBOW ?

"Look!" said Beth. "Someone's been painting the sky!"
Beth's granny came to the window. She saw a beautiful rainbow arching over the fields in front of their house.
"Isn't it lovely?" she said to Beth, and they looked at it for a long time.

"Gran," said Beth, "what is a rainbow?"
Beth's gran had lots of stories. She loved to tell stories from long ago.
"Well," she said, "hundreds and hundreds of years ago, people used to say the rainbow was a bridge between earth and heaven."
"Did people go across the bridge?" asked Beth.
"Not ordinary people. But gods did. The people in those days were called Vikings, and they believed in lots of powerful gods living up in the sky. The rainbow was there so that the Viking gods could gallop across to earth when they wanted to, and then back home again. Can't you just see them, on their big white horses with their swords and helmets flashing in the sun?"
Gran went off to finish making the tea.

28

Discussion: rainbows

Which explanations do you think are fiction and which is fact? Why? Which do you like best? Why?
Why do you think that people in the past thought up stories to explain rainbows? Do you know of any other rainbow stories?
(e.g. the crock of gold at the end of the rainbow)
(See also poem in Book 2, page 24, and accompanying notes on follow-up.)

> Science link: formulating hypotheses

Writing

Invent a story to explain a sort of weather.
Think up the idea first: characters/explanation.
Draw/paint a picture of the main event in the story.
Write the story to go with it, remembering structure (use poster or board notes suggested on page 97 of these Notes), and adding detail especially to the middle section (ref. to second poster or board notes).

(page 29)

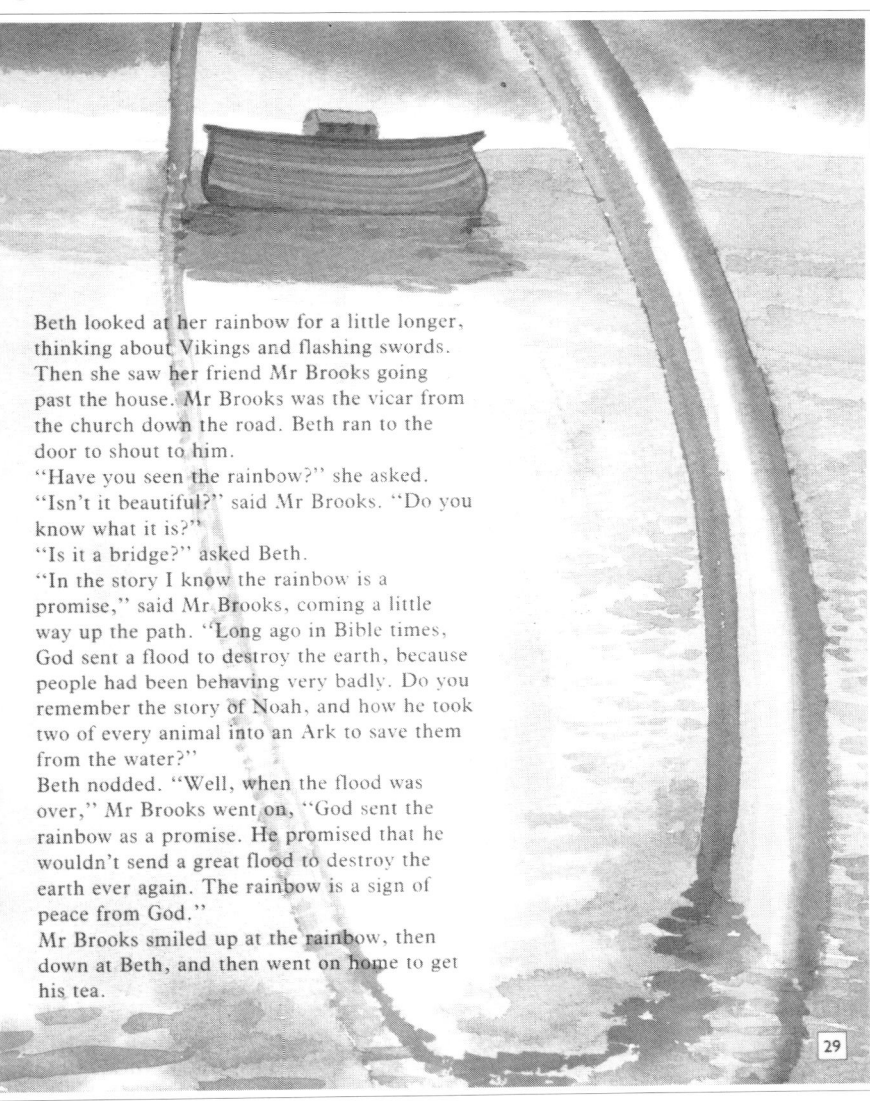

Beth looked at her rainbow for a little longer, thinking about Vikings and flashing swords. Then she saw her friend Mr Brooks going past the house. Mr Brooks was the vicar from the church down the road. Beth ran to the door to shout to him.
"Have you seen the rainbow?" she asked.
"Isn't it beautiful?" said Mr Brooks. "Do you know what it is?"
"Is it a bridge?" asked Beth.
"In the story I know the rainbow is a promise," said Mr Brooks, coming a little way up the path. "Long ago in Bible times, God sent a flood to destroy the earth, because people had been behaving very badly. Do you remember the story of Noah, and how he took two of every animal into an Ark to save them from the water?"
Beth nodded. "Well, when the flood was over," Mr Brooks went on, "God sent the rainbow as a promise. He promised that he wouldn't send a great flood to destroy the earth ever again. The rainbow is a sign of peace from God."
Mr Brooks smiled up at the rainbow, then down at Beth, and then went on home to get his tea.

Use of English: apostrophe

Because there is a great deal of direct speech, the apostrophe to show shortened forms is used frequently in this story:

p. 27 "Someone's been painting the sky! Isn't it lovely?"
"Can't you just see them?"

p. 28 "Isn't it beautiful?"
"he wouldn't send a great flood…"

p. 29 "That rainbow's a smasher, isn't it?"
"It happens when there's rain and sun… that's what it is."
etc.

Pupils can find the examples in the story and work out their full forms (e.g. Someone has been painting the sky!). Write shortened forms next to full forms on board, for pupils to work out (orally) the rule for where the apostrophe should be placed: i.e. where the letter(s) is missed out. Pupils can then look for more examples in other stories and poems.

Group reading

Once pupils are familiar with the story, it can be split up among various readers to be read almost like a play:
Reader 1 – Beth (this reader reads all the words actually spoken by Beth throughout the story)
Reader 2 – Narrator/gran (reads the rest of the first two sections)
Reader 3 – Narrator/Mr Brooks (reads the rest of the third section)
Reader 4 – Narrator/dad (reads the rest of the fourth section)
Reader 5 – Narrator/Sam (reads the rest of the final section).
Pupils' attention should be drawn to punctuation and expression.

Poem

Boats sail on the rivers,
    And ships sail on the seas;
But clouds that sail across the sky
    Are prettier far than these

There are bridges on the rivers,
    As pretty as you please;
But the bow that bridges heaven,
    And overtops the trees,
And builds a road from earth to sky,
    Is prettier far than these.
               (Christina Rossetti)

(page 30)

Language: a range of sentence connectives

Sentences can be connected in many ways: sometimes through vocabulary (e.g. 'Beth called to Sam. The little boy came trotting out.'); sometimes through layout (e.g. several sentences grouped as a paragraph); sometimes by grammatical features (e.g. linking pronouns, adverbial phrases of space and time, conjunctions, etc.). Pupils' skill in using and varying sentence connectives is usually a reflection of the extent of their reading rather than the result of teaching. However, the more aware children are of how language works and can be manipulated, the more likely they are to develop a wide range of strategies.

> Beth sat on the front step and looked at her rainbow again. After a while, her dad came up the path.
> "Hello, pet," he said. "That rainbow's a smasher, isn't it?"
> "Yes, but is it a bridge or a promise?" asked Beth.
> "Has Gran been telling you her stories again?" said dad, with a smile.
> "A rainbow is just sunlight shining on water. It happens when there's rain and sunshine in the air at the same time. The sunlight shines on the tiny raindrops, which splits the light up into lots of different colours. Light and water, that's what it is."
> Dad went off to wash his hands ready for tea.
>
> Beth counted on her fingers. Everybody seemed to think something different.
> Just then, her little brother Sam came trotting to the door.
> He looked up at the sky and his mouth fell open. "What is it?" he said.
> "What do you think it is?" Beth asked him.
> Sam thought for a moment.
> "I fink it's lovely," said Sam. He took Beth's hand so they could look at it together.
> "Yes," said Beth, "You're right, Sam. It's just lovely." And she took him inside to have his tea.

Worksheet 3j: joining sentences

This worksheet provides discussion material on some of the different ways sentences can be linked using 'joining words'. The 'joining words' should be cut out, as well as the pairs of sentences (as they are required). Sentences and joining words can then be moved about and tried in various combinations.

Teachers should supervise work on possible ways of joining the pairs of sentences. Pupils should then work in pairs to find as many variations as possible for joining the other pairs (jotting them down as they find them). The exercise can be turned into a team competition, and extra marks allotted for correct punctuation of jottings.

Books

Picture book:
Once Upon A Rainbow, Gabrielle El Chenaur and Naomi Lewis (Cape)

Story, which pupils nearing Level 3 could read for themselves:
'The Last Slice of Rainbow' from *The Last Slice of Rainbow and Other Stories,* Joan Aiken (Puffin)

Read aloud story:
'The Rainbow' from *Rainbow Tales,* Alison Uttley (Pan Books)

3j

Weather is full of the nicest sounds *(page 31)*

Weather is Full of the Nicest Sounds

Weather is full
of the nicest sounds:
it sings
and rustles
and pings
and pounds
and hums
and tinkles
and strums
and twangs
and whishes
and sprinkles
and splishes
and bangs
and mumbles
and grumbles
and rumbles
and flashes
and crashes.

I wonder
if thunder
frightens a bee,
a mouse in her house,
a bird in a tree?
A bear
or a hare
or a fish in the sea?

Not me!

Aileen Fisher

(Readability: Level 3)
Most children working towards Level 3 will need to hear the poem read several times (following in their books, if possible) before they can begin to join in the reading with any fluency, or to work with the poem on their own.

Reading/Discussion
Read the poem through with the children, and discuss as appropriate, e.g. *Do you think these noises frighten the animals? What weather noises do you think are frightening?* etc.

Group presentation/Taping a poem
The poem is suitable for taping with sound effects. Take the weather noises a few at a time and talk about what each one sounds like, and the sorts of weather they are associated with.

(Technology link)

Can you make a 'rustling' sound? What sort of weather might 'hum'? etc.

(Science link: production and transmission of sound)

Discuss how the sounds could be made, the sorts of things they could use to make them (e.g. paper, musical instruments, other items in the classroom, their hands, voices, etc.). Pupils then work in groups of about 4/5 to produce a taped reading of the poem accompanied by sounds. Encourage plenty of rehearsal before taping the presentation.

Language
All the 'sound words' in the poem are verbs. Can pupils recognise them? Can they say which tense they are in?
Compile a list of some more weather verbs, e.g.: the wind **blows**, the rain **falls**, the sun **shines**, the snowflakes **float**, etc.
Try converting the verbs in the poem into the past tense, e.g. 'It sang, and rustled, and pinged...'.

Story book
Might be suitable as a group reading book for pupils nearing Level 3, so that pupils share the reading with teacher support: *Rain and Shine,* Paul Rogers (Young Lions)

Glossaries (page 32)

The glossaries are provided to ensure that vocabulary needed for Level 3 work is available to pupils. Definitions are, as far as possible, in language appropriate to the age-group, and are therefore somewhat simplistic. (We often provide a more complex definition in later books.) Some terms, such as 'capital letter' and 'full stop' are not included, as we have assumed that pupils are already familiar with them.

All definitions require plenty of discussion with the teacher. Pupils must then experience the concept concerned within the context of real language before they can be expected to grasp the meaning. Wherever possible, vocabulary has been introduced in the Teacher's Notes to individual pages, often with follow-up in an exercise or worksheet.

By the time pupils have finished the book, they should be familiar with most of the terms.

GLOSSARY of words about reading and writing

- **abbreviation**
  A short way of writing something, often using initials, e.g. the letters *e.g.* mean *for example*.
- **browsing**
  Looking through books to get an idea of what they are about.
- **caption**
  Words written underneath a picture, to tell you about it.
- **diagram**
  A simple picture which helps to explain something clearly.
- **draft**
  A writer's try at expressing what he/she wants to say. The draft can then be edited and improved.
- **edit**
  To change or correct a piece of writing to make it better.
- **fable**
  A short story which teaches you a lesson or moral.
- **fiction**
  A story which is invented.
- **glossary**
  A list of difficult words, with their meanings, usually arranged in alphabetical order. You sometimes find a glossary at the back of a **non-fiction** book.
- **heading**
  The title at the top of a piece of writing, or at the beginning of a chapter in a book.
- **index**
  An alphabetical list at the back of a non-fiction book. It lists **key words** for all the topics in the book, and tells which pages contain information about each topic.
- **key words**
  The important words about a particular topic, e.g. the words in this **glossary** are key words about reading and writing.
- **non-fiction**
  Facts.
- **notes**
  You write notes to help you remember something. They are short, quick reminders and they do not have to be in sentences.
- **reference books**
  Books which you use to look up particular bits of information. You do not read them from beginning to end.
- **scanning**
  Looking quickly over pages to find particular key words.
- **skimming**
  Looking quickly over pages of a book to get an idea of what they are about.
- **sub-heading**
  The title given to one section of a longer piece of writing. There may be several sub-headings under one main **heading** or chapter-heading.
- **summary**
  A short description of the main points of something.
- **word processor**
  A computer used for writing.

32

Suggestions for introducing new words

abbreviation: note the use of 'e.g.' in many glossary notes. Collect other common abbreviations and their meanings.
consonant: see 'vowel'
glossary: do any books in the project collection have glossaries?
word family: collect families on the basis of the examples given.

(page 33)

GLOSSARY of words about language

♦ **adjective**
A describing word, e.g. *hot, wet, windy.*

♦ **apostrophe**
A punctuation mark like a flying comma. It shows where letters have been missed out of a word or words, e.g. *didn't* (short for did not), *I've* (short for I have).

♦ **consonant**
Any letter of the alphabet which is not a vowel, i.e. B, C, D, F, G, H, J, K, L, M, N, P, Q, R, S, T, V, W, X, Y, Z.

♦ **joining word**
A word which joins groups of words together, e.g. *and, but, when, so, as, because.* It can be used to join two sentences together to make one sentence, e.g.
The sun grew hotter. I felt tired.
1. The sun grew hotter *and* I felt tired.
2. *As* the sun grew hotter, I felt tired.
3. I felt tired *because* the sun grew hotter.

♦ **noun**
A naming word – the name of a person, place, animal or thing, e.g. *boy, city, horse, ship.*

♦ **part of speech**
The job a word is doing in a phrase or sentence, e.g. noun, verb, adjective, pronoun, joining word.

♦ **phrase**
A group of words which go together, but do not make a complete sentence.

♦ **plural**
See singular and plural.

♦ **proper noun**
The special name of a particular person, place, animal or thing, e.g. *Frank, London, Black Beauty, Queen Mary.* Proper nouns always begin with a capital letter.

♦ **pronoun**
A word which stands in place of a noun. The most common pronouns are: *I/me/my, you/your, he/him/his, she/her, it/its, we/our, they/them/their.*

♦ **punctuation marks**
These help a reader make sense of a piece of writing. Some show how words are grouped together to make sense (e.g. comma and full stop). Some also show the tone of voice you should use (e.g. question mark).

♦ **questions and statements**
Sentences can be questions or statements. A question-sentence asks something and it ends with a question mark, e.g. *What is your favourite weather?*
A statement-sentence is an ordinary sentence and it ends with a full stop, e.g. *My favourite weather is sunshine.*

♦ **sentence**
A group of words that go together to make complete sense. A sentence always contains at least one verb. It begins with a capital letter and ends with a full stop.

♦ **singular and plural**
Nouns can be either singular or plural.
Singular = just one,
plural = more than one,
e.g. *rainbow* (sing.), *rainbows* (pl.)
child (sing.), *children* (pl.)

♦ **tense**
Verbs can be in the past, present or future tenses, e.g. past – *the wind blew*, present – *the wind blows*, future – *the wind will blow.*

♦ **verb**
A doing word, e.g. *blow, fall, be.*

♦ **vowel**
One of these five letters of the alphabet: A, E, I, O, U. (The letter y is a 'part-time vowel', sometimes standing in for the sound of 'i').

♦ **word family**
A group of words that come from the same root e.g.
1. *rain* (noun), *rained* (verb)
rainy (adjective), *rainbow* (noun).
2. parts of the verb 'to blow':
blow, blown, blowing, blew.

Words about language
At Book 3 Level the development of pupil's awareness of language as a system becomes important. This necessitates the introduction of many metalinguistic terms, which we have presented in a separate glossary. We hope that the separation will help children grasp that some words are related to how we use language, while others are the specialised vocabulary required to talk about language (just as we need specialised vocabulary to talk about Maths).

Language: metalinguistic terms
A way of checking that pupils are familiar with this vocabulary is to copy the words and their definitions on to separate pieces of card and ask pupils to match them up correctly.

Punctuation marks
(NB The definition given here does not cover the use of the apostrophe in contractions – the apostrophe is always a rogue punctuation mark.)
Punctuation at this stage is related mainly to sentence punctuation and practice is given in **Worksheet 3h**. Another useful activity for sensitising pupils to punctuation is the 'Talking punctuation game'.

Talking punctuation game
Assign a sound to each punctuation mark in a particular passage.
(e.g. for the letter on page 27:

full stop	=	'splat'
question mark	=	'boing'
exclamation mark	=	'thwack'
comma	=	clicking noise with the tongue
capital letter	=	'Hrrumph', immediately before the capital)

Ask one child to read the letter aloud slowly, while the rest of the group, guided by the teacher, make the punctuation noises.

Punctuation marks are dealt with again in Books 4 and 5, and the subject is given more comprehensive treatment there.

In the Sun/Winter Days (back cover)

Poems/Reading/Discussion

Read the poems and discuss as appropriate.

e.g.: *In what sort of voice/at what speed do you think 'In the Sun' should be read? What about 'Winter Days'?*

Pair pupils and let them try ways of reading both poems to achieve maximum effect. Some could present their readings to the class, for discussion of the most successful.

Science links: seasonal variations; temperature.

Comparison

Look back to 'Summer and Winter' on page 2 of Book 3. *Which do you prefer – that poem or these two? Why?*

Possible lead-in to a discussion of the value of expansion of ideas/descriptive writing.

Language

In 'In the Sun', the verbs are particularly important. *What are they, and how does the poet give them special importance?*

In the second verse of 'Winter Days' find four nouns and four adjectives.

Poetry/Discussion

Give pupils time to look back over all the poems in the Pupil's Book, and hear them all read aloud again.

Which is your favourite? Which is your least favourite?

Encourage pupils to give reasons each time. Perhaps you could compile a 'Top 10' list of poems.

Books

Non-fiction picture book:
Summer and Winter, Heather Amery and Peter Firmin (Usborne)

Read alone stories:
Level 2 – *Frog and Toad All Year,* Arnold Lobel (Puffin I Can Read Books)
Nearing Level 3 – *Tom, Zak and Emmie in Winter,* Amy Erlich (A & C Black)

Picture books:
The Selfish Giant, Oscar Wilde/Michael Foreman and Freire Wright (Picture Puffin)
The Tiny Seed, Eric Carle (Hodder & Stoughton)

Prediction/Discussion material

The Twelve Months

A story from Czechoslovakia

Once upon a time there was a young girl called Marushka. She lived in a cottage near the forest with her cruel stepmother, who made her do all the work. The stepmother had a daughter of her own, Holena, who was lazy and greedy, and who ordered Marushka around as though she were a servant.

In spite of her hard life, Marushka was always cheerful and good-tempered, and it showed in her face. She had a pretty, smiling mouth and warm, friendly eyes. This made her stepmother jealous, because Holena had a selfish, puckered little face and a sly, greedy look. The stepmother began to worry in case Marushka grew up to be more beautiful than her own daughter.

At last the wicked stepmother thought of a way to be rid of Marushka. One day in January, when the snow was lying all around the cottage, she called the girl to her. 'I want some violets,' she said. 'They would brighten up the cottage.' 'But it's winter, stepmother', said Marushka. 'Violets don't grow in the cold weather.'

'Don't argue with me, girl,' the stepmother cried. 'Go out and pick me some violets. And don't come back until you've got some!'

Poor Marushka put on her warmest shawl and went out into the snow. She wandered into the forest to look for violets, but she knew there was no chance of finding any.

Eventually, when she was freezing cold and near to despair, she saw a light shining deep in the forest. She went towards it, and, in a clearing, she found a fire burning on a mound. Seated around it on twelve rocks were twelve men. Three of the men were young and handsome, three were not quite so young, three were a lot older, and the last three were ancient and harsh-looking with long white beards. One of these last three was seated on a specially high rock, holding a wooden staff. He seemed to be the leader.

Marushka was rather frightened of the men, but she was also terribly cold. She approached them quietly and spoke politely to the old man on the highest rock: 'Please, sir, would you mind if I warmed myself for a little while at your fire?'

The old man turned his stern face towards her and studied her for a while. At last he said, 'Very well, my child, come forward.' Marushka went into the centre of the circle and stood by the fire.

'What are you doing wandering in the forest in this cold weather?' the old man asked her.

Marushka explained how her stepmother had sent her out to find violets.

'But it is deep mid-winter,' said the old man. 'Violets will not grow in the snow.'

'I know, sir,' said Marushka, 'but my stepmother will not let me return home until I find some. I beg you, if you know where I can find some violets, please tell me.'

Now the twelve men were, in fact, the twelve months of the year, and the old man who had spoken to Marushka was January. He was sitting on the high rock because it was his turn to rule the world. But he felt sorry for the girl, so he turned to his youngest brother, March, and said: 'Come, March, take my place for a few minutes.'

March smiled and stood up. He took the wooden staff from January's hand, waved it over the fire and took his brother's place on the high rock. Immediately the snow around them melted, buds began to appear on the trees, and a few spring flowers began to push through the green grass. 'Quickly, child, gather some violets,' said March. Marushka did not understand what was happening, but she quickly gathered a bunch of young fresh violets and thanked the men. Then January returned to his place and all was bleak and cold as it had been before. Marushka hurried home with her little bunch of flowers.

The cruel stepmother was amazed to see violets in January, and asked Marushka where she had got them. But all the girl would say was that she had gathered them in the forest. Her stepmother stormed away, fuming, to think of another plan.

'Marushka,' she said the next day, 'you did well to find the violets. Today I feel like some strawberries for my dinner. Go and gather me some.'

There was nothing Marushka could say to persuade her stepmother that strawberries would not be found in the snow, and again she found herself freezing cold and wandering in the forest.

Again, after several hours of wandering, she spotted the glow of the fire in a clearing. She was back where the twelve strange men sat up on their rocks. Again she went hesitantly up to them and asked permission to warm herself by the fire.

January asked why she had returned to the forest in the freezing weather, and Marushka explained. When he heard her story, January looked very stern. He turned to one of his not-quite-so-young brothers. 'July,' he said, 'Take my place for a few minutes.'

July smiled kindly at Marushka, took the staff from his white-haired brother, waved it in the fire and sat down on the high rock. Again the snow disappeared, and instead the earth lay warm in the sunshine. Flowers bloomed everywhere, and the air was filled with the humming of summer insects. Marushka found a wild strawberry bush thick with fruit and quickly picked enough to fill her apron. Then July returned the staff to his brother and went back to his place. And the few moments' summer gave way to winter again.

When Marushka arrived home with her apron full of strawberries her stepmother and Holena were beside themselves with amazement and fury. The girl would tell them nothing except that she had found the fruit in the forest. So the next day her stepmother tried again. 'I should like an apple to finish my meal today,' she said to Marushka, 'and Holena would like one too. Go and find us two ripe apples in your wonderful forest. There should not be many apples in the snow.'

This time Marushka went straight to the clearing, apologised to the brothers for disturbing them and explained again what had happened. January frowned even more deeply when he heard her story, and at once called September, one of the older brothers, to take his place. September waved the staff over the fire and sat on the high rock. Immediately the weather changed to a misty autumn day, with a slight chill in the air. The leaves on the trees became rich shades of orange and yellow, and on a branch near Marushka hung two beautiful ripe red apples. She plucked them quickly and thanked the brothers, who returned to their places. Then she hurried off home.

When Holena and her mother saw the apples they were angrier than ever. 'You have found a treasure of fruit and flowers,' cried the stepmother, 'but you will not tell us where it is!'

'You are greedy and mean,' said Holena. 'Why did you bring us only two apples?'

'There were only two apples,' said Marushka.

'Nonsense,' said Holena. 'I bet there are thousands and you want to keep them all for yourself. Tell us where you found them. I will go and get some myself.'

Marushka was forced to tell them the way to the clearing where the brothers sat, and she watched miserably as Holena dressed in her warmest furs and set off into the forest.

Pause to ask: What do you think happened next? What hints in the story so far help you reach your conclusion? Discussion of characters, the form of the story, the likelihood of a happy/unhappy ending.

When Holena arrived at the clearing, she didn't hang back shyly as Marushka had done. She marched straight in and, without asking permission, she warmed her hands at the brothers' fire. Then she turned to January and said, 'All right, grandad, how do I get my hands on all these flowers and fruits you've been giving to my stepsister?' Then January knew who she was, and his stern old face darkened with anger. He picked up his staff and waved it across the flames.

Immediately the harsh January weather became crueller and colder than Holena had ever known it. A terrible blizzard raged through the forest, the girl's body froze like ice, and she fell dead on the ground.

When her beloved daughter did not return, Marushka's stepmother went out into the forest to look for her. But January's fierce blizzard was still raging, and the woman was frozen to death before she even reached the clearing.

So Marushka was left alone at home to look after the house, free from the bullying and cruelty of her stepmother and stepsister, until eventually she married a miller in the nearby town and settled down to live happily ever after. Her children loved to hear the story of how she was sent into the forest on three impossible quests, and how the kindness of the twelve months helped her to survive.

> Science links: effects of weather on environment; effects of temperature on human beings; seasonal variations.

Discussion

Were the predictions accurate? How did people decide on their predictions? What is the 'moral' or lesson of the story? What sort of personality was Marushka/her stepmother/Holena? What adjectives could you use to describe them?
Would you say the Twelve Months were kind or cruel? Give reasons for your answer.

Drama/Writing

The story is suitable for dramatisation. If playscripts are to be produced, use the layout for 'The Rat King' as a model.

Make a snowflake

1. Fold a piece of A4 paper in half lengthways to make a long thin rectangle.
2. Find the centre of the fold and mark it.
3. Measure 9cm from the top left-hand corner and mark it. Draw a line to join the two marks. 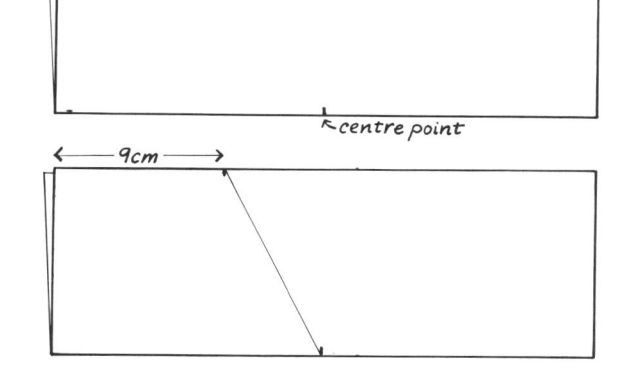 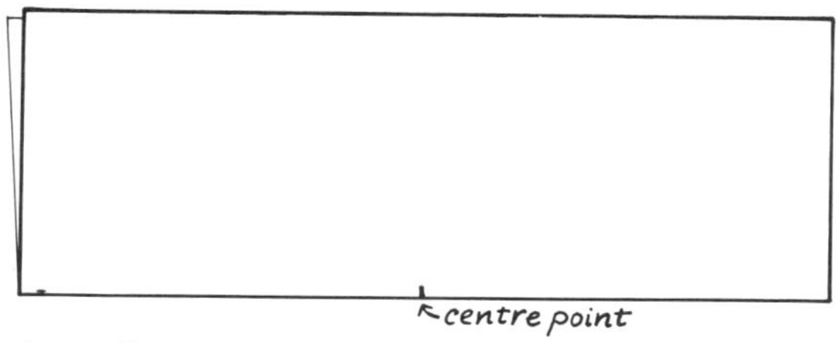
4. Fold the bottom right-hand side up to lie along the line you have drawn. 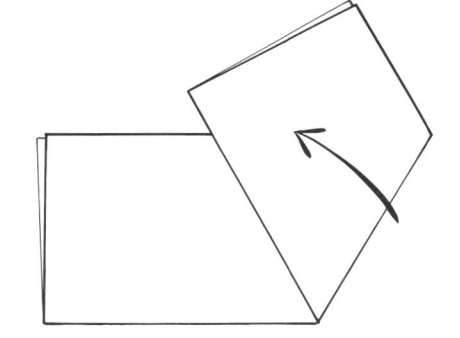
5. Fold the bottom left-hand side over the top meet the right-hand fold. 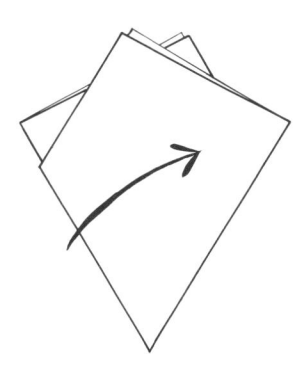
6. Cut along dots. 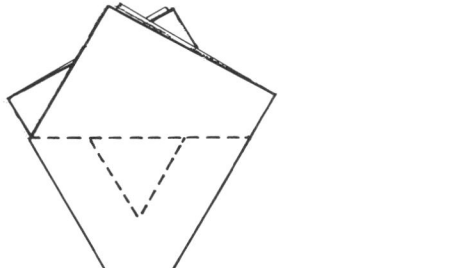
7. Cut out patterns if wished. 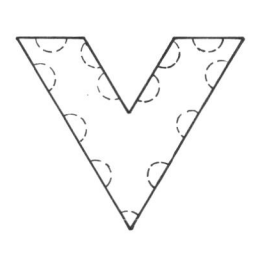
8. Open out and display.

Weather non-fiction books for Key Stage 1

Here is a list of non-fiction/reference books which will support your topic in the classroom. The emphasis is on books which will appeal to the children and which they will be able to use themselves.

ARDLEY, N, *My science book of weather*, Dorling Kindersley 1992 (0863187978)
BARRETT, N, *Hurricanes and tornadoes*, Franklin Watts 1989 (0863138810)
*BOLWELL, L H, *What's the weather like? It's raining*, Wayland 1985 (0850785138)
BOLWELL, L H, *What's the weather like? It's snowing*, Wayland 1985 (0850785413)
BOLWELL, L H, *What's the weather like? It's sunny*, Wayland 1985 (0850785146)
BOLWELL, L H, *What's the weather like? It's windy*, Wayland 1985 (0850785421)
*BOLWELL, L & LINES, C, *Climate and weather*, Wayland 1984 (0850784174)
BOWER, M, *Experiment with weather*, Two Can 1992 (1854341243)
BROWN, J & R, *Weather*, Belitha Press 1991 (1855610647)
BUTLER, D, *Changing seasons*, Simon & Schuster 1990 (0750002913)
CATHERALL, E, *The weather*, Wayland 1986 (08500788609)
CATHERALL, E, *Wind play*, Wayland 1986 (0850787149)
DAVIES, K & OLDFIELD, W, *Weather*, Wayland 1991 (0780200006)
FARNDON, J, *Weather*, Dorling Kindersley 1992 (0863188257)
JACKMAN, W, *Weather*, Wayland 1991 (0750200944)
LANGTHORNE, J & CONROY, G, *Weather and climate*, Wayland 1992 (0750203153)
LLEWELLYN, C, *In the air*, Simon & Schuster 1991 (0750006110)
MATTHEWS, S, *Weather*, Moonlight 1990 (1851030859)
PALMER, J, *Rain*, Franklin Watts 1992 (0749606428)
PALMER, J, *Snow*, Franklin Watts 1992 (0749606436)
POWELL, J, *Rainy weather*, Wayland 1992 (0750205059)
POWELL, J, *Snowy weather*, Wayland 1992 (0750205075)
POWELL, J, *Sunny weather*, Wayland 1992 (0750205040)
POWELL, J, *Windy weather*, Wayland 1992 (0750205067)
Rain, Macdonald 1986 (0356035425)
RICHARDSON, J, *The seasons*, Franklin Watts 1991 (0749607297)
RICHARDSON, J, *The weather*, Franklin Watts 1992 (0749607823) •
ROGERS, D, *Rain*, Angus & Robertson 1980 (0207138087)
SWALLOW, S, *Water*, Franklin Watts 1990 (0749602295)
TAYLOR, B, *Wind and weather*, Franklin Watts 1991 (0749604468)
*VERDET, J P, *The air around us*, Moonlight 1986 (1851030050)
Weather, Macdonald 1975 (0356051307)

*These titles are unfortunately 'out of print' but should be available through your local library service.

Programmes of Study for Key Stage 1, England and Wales

Speaking and Listening

Through the programme of study, pupils should encounter a range of situations, audiences and activities which are designed to develop their competence, precision and confidence in speaking and listening, irrespective of their initial competence or home language.

These planned situations and activities should cover:
- working with other children and adults – involving discussion with others; listening to, and giving weight to, the opinions of others; perceiving the relevance of contributions; timing contributions; adjusting and adapting to views expressed;
- development of listening (and, as appropriate, reactive) skills in non-reciprocal situations, *e.g. radio programmes*;
- development of speaking and listening skills both when role-playing and otherwise – when describing experiences, expressing opinions, articulating personal feelings and formulating and making appropriate responses to increasingly complex instructions and questions;
- development, by informal means and in the course of purposeful activities, of pupils' powers of concentration, grasp of turn-taking, ability to gain and hold the attention of their listeners, and ability to voice disagreement courteously with an opposing point of view.

All activities should:
- help to develop in pupils' speaking and listening, their grasp of sequence, cause and effect, reasoning, sense of consistency, clarity of argument, appreciation of relevance and irrelevance, and powers of prediction and recall;
- by informal and indirect means, develop pupils' ability to adjust the language they use and its delivery to suit particular audiences, purposes and contexts and, when listening to others, to respond to different ways of talking in different contexts and for different purposes. Pupils should therefore be encouraged to reflect on and evaluate their use of spoken language and to reformulate it to help the listener;
- draw on examples from across the curriculum, and in particular those existing requirements for mathematics and science which refer to use of spoken language and vocabulary, asking questions, working in groups, explaining and presenting ideas, giving and understanding instructions;
- include provision for pupils to talk and listen in groups of different sizes and to a range of audiences;
- emphasise the importance of clear diction and audibility.

Reading

Reading activities should build on the oral language and experiences which pupils bring from home. Teaching should cover a range of rich and stimulating texts, both fiction and non-fiction, and should ensure that pupils regularly hear stories, told or read aloud, and hear and share poetry read by the teacher and each other.

Reading should include picture books, nursery rhymes, poems, folktales, myths, legends and other literature which takes account of pupils' linguistic competences and backgrounds. Both boys and girls should experience a wide range of children's literature. Non-fiction texts should include those closely related to the world of the child and extend to those which enable children to deepen an understanding of themselves and the world in which they live, *e.g. books about weather, wildlife, other countries, food, transport, the stars.*

Pupils should encounter an environment in which they are surrounded by books and other reading material presented in an attractive and inviting way. The reading material should include material which relates to the real world, such as labels, captions, notices, children's newspapers, books of instructions, plans and maps, diagrams, computer printout and visual display.

Pupils' own writing – either independently written, or stories dictated to the teacher or composed in collaboration with other pupils – should form part of the resources for reading.

Teachers should take account of the important link between home and school, actively encouraging parents to participate and share in their child's reading, and supporting pupils where this is not possible.

Detailed provisions
Activities should ensure that pupils:
- hear books, stories and poems read aloud or on radio, tape or television and take part in shared reading experiences with other pupils and the teacher, using texts composed and dictated by the pupils themselves, as well as rhymes, poems, songs and familiar stories (including traditional stories from a variety of cultures);
- read in the context of role-play and dramatic play, *e.g. in the home play corner, class shop, or other dramatic play setting such as a cafe, hospital or post office. Such reading might include a menu, a sign on a door, a label on a packet, or a sign above a counter.* For pupils working towards level 1, the settings should include individual letters, *e.g. 'P' for Parking*, and individual words, *e.g. 'Exit'*, which pupils can be encouraged to recognise;
- retell, re-read or dramatise familiar stories and poems;
- make their own books about particular experiences, areas of interest or personal stories, *e.g. guide books, instructions, favourite poems or stories*;
- talk to the teacher and each other about the books and stories they have been reading or listening to;
- widen their range of reading, turning readily to books, choosing those which they would like to hear or read and saying why;
- ask and answer questions about what has been heard or read - how characters feel, their motives, the endings of stories;
- talk about the ways in which language is written down, in shared reading or writing sessions or in discussion with the teacher, identify words, phrases, patterns of letters and other features of written language which they recognise, and notice how words are constructed and spelled;
- refer to information books, dictionaries, word books or simple data on computers as a matter of course. Pupils should be encouraged to formulate first the questions they need to answer by using such sources, so that they use them effectively and do not simply copy verbatim;
- talk about the content of information texts.

Through the programme of study pupils should be guided so as to:
- appreciate the significance of print and the fact that pictures and other visual media can also convey meaning, *e.g. road signs, logos*;
- build up, in the context of their reading, a vocabulary of words recognised on sight;
- use the available cues, such as pictures, context, phonic cues, word shapes and meaning of a passage to decipher new words;
- be ready to make informed guesses, and to correct themselves in the light of additional information, *e.g. by reading ahead or looking back in the text*;
- develop the capacity to convey, when reading aloud, the meaning of the text clearly to the listener through intonation and phrasing;
- develop the habit of silent reading.

Writing, Spelling and Handwriting

Pupils should have frequent opportunities to write in different contexts and for a variety of purposes and audiences, including for themselves.

Pupils should write in a wide range of activities. Early 'play' writing, *e.g. in a play house, class shop, office, hospital,* should be encouraged and respected.

Pupils will have seen different kinds of writing in the home – their names on birthday cards or letters, forms, shopping lists and so on. Those whose parents are literate in a language other than English may have observed writing in their own first language, for which there may be a different writing system. Such awareness of writing in any form can help pupils to understand some of the functions of written language and should be used to promote their understanding of the functions of the English writing system.

Pupils should see adults writing. Teachers should write alongside pupils, sharing and talking about their writing, *e.g. in journals, notes and diagrams,* so that the range of uses of writing is brought out. Pupils should be made aware of how pieces of work they have produced relate to adult uses of writing.

Detailed provisions

Pupils should be taught the conventional ways of forming letter shapes, lower case and capitals, through purposeful guided practice in order to foster a comfortable and legible handwriting style.

Pupils should be enabled to compose at greater length than they can manage to write down by themselves, by:
- dictating to their teacher or another adult, or into a tape recorder; or
- working with other children; or
- using a word processor. Pupils should be able to produce copies of work drafted on a computer, and encouraged to incorporate the print-out in other work, including displays.

As they become familiar with the conventions of writing, pupils should be introduced to the most common spelling patterns of consonant and short vowel sounds. Pupils should be taught how to spell words which occur frequently in their writing, or which are important to them, and those which exemplify regular spelling patterns. They should be encouraged to spell words for themselves, and to remember the correct spelling, *e.g. by compiling their own list of words they have used.* They should be taught the names and order of the letters of the alphabet.

Pupils should:
- undertake a range of chronological writing including some at least of diaries, stories, letters, accounts of tasks they have done and of personal experiences, records of observations they have made, *e.g. in a science or design activity,* and instructions, *e.g. recipes;*
- undertake a range of non-chronological writing which includes, for pupils working towards **level 2**, some at least of lists, captions, labels, invitations, greeting cards, notices, posters and, for pupils working towards **level 3**, plans and diagrams, descriptions, *e.g. of a person or place,* and notes for an activity, *e.g. in science and designing and making;*
- play with language, for example by making up jingles, poems, word games, riddles, and games which involve word and spelling patterns.

Pupils should write individually and in age groups, sharing their writing with others and discussing what they have written, and should produce finished pieces of work for wider audiences, *e.g. stories, newspapers, magazines, books, games and guides for other children.*

Pupils should be asked to write in response to a range of well chosen stories, poems, plays or television programmes.

Pupils should discuss their writing frequently, talking about the varied types and purposes of writing, *e.g. list, poem, story, recipe*. Teachers should talk about correct spelling and its patterns, about punctuation, and should introduce pupils to terms such as punctuation, letter, capital letter, full stop, question mark.

Pupils should be taught to help the reader by leaving a space between words and by ending sentences with a full stop or question mark and by beginning them with a capital letter.

Pupils working towards **level 3** should be taught to recognise that writing involves:
- decision making - when the context (the specific situation, precise purpose and intended audience) is established;
- planning - when initial thoughts and the framework are recorded and ordered;
- drafting - when initial thoughts are developed, evaluated and reshaped by expansion, addition or amendment to the text.

They should be taught to look for instances where:
- ideas should be differently ordered or more fully expressed in order to convey their meaning;
- tenses or pronouns have been used incorrectly or inconsistently;
- meaning is unclear because of insufficient punctuation or omitted words;
- meaning would be improved by a richer or more precise choice of vocabulary.

They should be taught, in the context of discussion about their own writing, grammatical terms such as sentence, verb, tense, noun, pronoun.

Programmes of Study for Scotland

Listening

Listening has implications for speech development, thinking, and learning generally. Though talking and listening often occur in proximity to each other (in, for example, discussion) they are separable for educational purposes and are regularly in practice - for example, listening to a talk, to a teacher, to radio, to a series of instructions.

In the early years, listening is the main means by which knowledge is acquired but teachers at all stages must be attentive to pupils' abilities and capacities, nurturing them in constructive, interesting ways, and noting and attending to specific problems which may impede the learning process. For pupils who may have difficulty in learning the skills of reading and writing, it is the oral components that will, perhaps, provide the main basis for thinking about experiences, expressing feelings and engaging with society.

Listening effectively is an active process. It has much to do with the knowledge and experience of the listener, with motivation and involvement, and with the individual situation in which listening takes place. People listen best when the information is of importance to them, when they have to take some action on it or have the opportunity to reply or participate. Listeners, therefore, have to learn to select relevant information from what they are hearing or seeing.

It cannot be assumed that children will have acquired the necessary skills - of concentrating, and of thinking about and recalling what they hear and see - by the age of 5: some may already possess good general alertness; others will not have acquired the basic habits; a few may reveal signs of physical difficulties in hearing which will require treatment.

In the early stages the pupils will:
- be encouraged to sit comfortably and quietly, face the source of the message and not interrupt; they will also begin to learn how to conduct themselves in discussion;
- regularly listen to good stories and particularly to tales and poems which incorporate the 'three Rs' of listening for young pupils - Repetitions, Rhythms and Rhymes; many of these will be of Scottish origin; some will be live performances by teacher or pupils; others will be audio or video recordings;
- engage in a programme linked to the early teaching of reading and writing, which will involve developing auditory discrimination and matching sounds with pictures, printed letters and words.

At all stages, in ways appropriate to their age and attainments, pupils will:
- work regularly in pairs or groups;
- undertake practical activities which give them an interesting purpose for their listening;
- listen to messages or narratives in order to predict at various stages likely outcomes and to locate with increasing accuracy genre, purposes and audience;
- play listening games and other activities designed to develop skills in attention and recall and the identification of sounds;
- use tape or video recorders to allow them to hear, watch and reflect upon what they themselves and their classmates have said;
- listen to speakers and to messages that employ Scottish language features;
- encounter a range of dialects and accents to enhance their linguistic competence and social confidence making use of radio, television, film, audio and video tapes, and song;

- discuss terms associated with knowledge about language where these help to clarify meaning;
- be given opportunities to associate listening with other forms of communication such as body language, music, set and costume designs;
- demonstrate a response to their listening in a variety of media-writing, pictures, graphics, speech and, performance.

Contexts for Listening as pupils get older will become more complex. There will be a corresponding need for listeners to be more aware of purposes and of the uses to which the listening is to be put. They will also be able to listen selectively at some times; pay close attention at other, more important times; adapt their mode of listening to their intention in listening; recognise the genre of the communication and be able to recall it. Assessment of listening should be varied. It would be wrong for a pupil's listening development to be stunted by asking for too much evidence of it in a component like writing which is still proving difficult.

Talking

Talking helps us sort out what we think and is the main means of social communication and interaction. It is through talking with peers, teachers and other adults that much of pupils' learning will occur. From the earliest stages, pupils should talk together about the issues within their common experience. Contexts for talking should be varied, with opportunities to discuss, to question, and to respond to books, other texts, and pupils' own talk and writing.

The whole curriculum offers a widening set of contexts for talk and it is through talk that the pupil makes sense of the range of ideas in that curriculum. Through personal experiences in and out of school, children should be encouraged to develop a growing awareness of the language appropriate to different audiences, purposes and situations.

Most children will have acquired skills in talking before they come to school, but teachers at the early stages will ensure that pupils are given opportunities to:
- learn the disciplines of effective talking - sitting comfortably, taking turns, keeping still and quiet, listening to the other speaker;
- talk in the reading and writing programme;
- use talk in structured play to arrive at outcomes.

At all stages, in ways appropriate to their age and attainments, pupils will:
- talk to peers, other pupils, teachers and adults in the context of their classwork;
- engage in practical activities which will require them to talk together to produce an outcome;
- make use of audio or video recorders to hear and to discuss their own and their classmates' performance;
- play games and engage in simulations and role-play, to develop their confidence and competence, and to facilitate talking;
- talk in Standard English, and their own dialect, as appropriate;
- give individual presentations to stimulate interest and command the attention of an audience;
- be given opportunities for talking in drama and performance;
- develop language awareness through talk and discussion.

Reading

Learning to read accurately and with discrimination becomes increasingly important as pupils move through their education. Reading and writing are reciprocal skills; attainment in one is usually paralleled by a similar attainment in the other; teaching one is closely related to teaching the other.

Pupils should be encouraged to read for enjoyment and, with support from the teacher, to maintain a personal reading programme. They should be helped to develop their own tastes in fiction and non-fiction and at the same time to gain confidence in speaking and writing about them. To foster this, it is essential that the class library is well stocked with colourful and interesting reading material.

The importance of meaning should be stressed at all stages. The activity of reading should take place, wherever possible, in an appropriate context, and it should be concerned with the gaining of meaning from a suitable text. Reading should always have a purpose which is clear to both the teacher and the pupil.

At the earliest stages learning to read is dependent upon the spoken language that pupils bring to school. It will also be influenced by the knowledge they have gained in the pre-school years about the conventions of print itself. Some pupils in P1 will be familiar with story-books, poems, nursery rhymes, and print in their environment; some may have already started to recognise single works and even letters. However, for many pupils the experience of hearing stories read aloud and talking about pictures will be encountered for the first time as part of the school's early reading programme. At this stage pupils will:
- be involved in pre-reading activities to develop skills of matching, discrimination, left-to-right eye movement, and sequencing;
- learn to enjoy books by listening to stories and talking about them;
- create and read short texts with teacher support;
- learn the basic skills of reading through a systematic and progressive programme.

As pupils' reading becomes less supported by illustrations, they must learn to recognise the commoner patterns in fiction and non-fiction. As texts become more complex and various in form, the teacher needs to deploy a widening range of techniques such as: sequencing, prediction, close procedure, evaluating the text, making deductions, marking text, comparing and contrasting different texts.

At later stages, reading activities should demand that pupils show an overall grasp of a text, and understanding of specific details and how they contribute to the whole, make inferences, supply appropriate supporting evidence and identify intended audience, purpose and features of style. In longer reading activities, for example novels, teaching the strategies which will help them to make sense of aspects such as plot, characters and themes is essential. In all of these activities, pupils will be helped by developing, through discussion, knowledge about language.

In teaching reading through all stages, in ways appropriate to pupils' ages and attainment, the teacher can focus on texts:
- before reading
- by priming pupils for the task, for example, by alerting them to unfamiliar content or ideas;
- by directing them into the task;
- during and after reading
- by providing questions which ask for literal, inferential and evaluative responses;
- by asking them to demonstrate understanding by doing or speaking;
- by asking readers to use the text as a model for their own writing.

Writing

Writing helps pupils to clarify their thoughts and experiences, and to give them personal meaning. Through writing, pupils can define, order and understand ideas. Because writing is essential for communication within society, it is important that pupils learn precision in its conventions.

Handwriting skills will be formally taught, especially in the early years. Later, pupils will pay attention to handwriting in the normal course of composing their own writing.

For the most part, writing will be developed in association with the other three components. Acquiring writing skills begins in the earliest years, and at all stages the teacher should be involved in listening, discussing, and assisting with the selection of ideas, overseeing content, organisation and form. The teacher will also demonstrate and require different writing strategies. For example, in producing writing the following strategy of drafting and re-drafting should be used:
- presenting ideas;
- discussing them with teacher and/or peers;
- selecting what is appropriate;
- developing them in expanded text (writing, drawings, storyboarding, word processing or simple flowcharts, as appropriate);
- discussing this with teacher and/or peers;
- producing a re-draft (which may be the final copy).

At the early stages, the teacher should respond to the content and structure of what is being written, leaving spelling and simple punctuation to the final draft. But with regular practice the pupil should be taught to give increasing priority to surface features of the text such as spelling, punctuation and presentation.

As pupils begin to read more widely so their writing will develop and become more varied. From writing about events drawn from their day-to-day lives they will write about matters which go beyond their real-life experiences. They will demonstrate that they can write for a larger number of audiences and purposes, and from points of view other than their own. They will attempt more complex narratives and will be asked to extend their ability to write non-narrative texts, for example, reports, letters and news items.

Teachers will, therefore, spend time devising programmes which will provide contexts in which pupils will be asked to write in a variety of forms. Pupils will also write for a number of readerships, in language registers and with degrees of formality that will depend on the writer's familiarity - which may be real or imaginary - with the target readership. In such programmes and contexts, teaching approaches, tasks and experiences will motivate and support pupils, especially those with special needs, as they gain a set of essential but complex skills.

The combination of purpose, form and readership will influence pupils' choice of appropriate language and they should be faced with tasks which clearly demand the use of a variety of styles. Mostly this will involve forms of Standard English, but from time to time the child's own dialect will also be used for appropriate purposes, and attention given to enriching it.